DeShazer

by C. Hoyt Watson

SALTBOX PRESS
SPRING ARBOR, MICHIGAN

DeShazer was first published in 1950 by the Light and Life Press, Winona Lake, Indiana. Author Charles Hoyt Watson was at that time President of Seattle Pacific College.

Published in Spring Arbor, Michigan by Saltbox Press. Distributed by Jacob DeShazer, 3943 47th Avenue, N.E., Salem, Oregon 97305

Printed in the United States of America
July, 1991
ISBN: 1-878559-00-1

Contents

Forward

Jacob DeShazer is "a man sent from God." You have here the story of an ordinary man, wholly dedicated to the mission of bringing a lost world to Christ. It is a story of "a bad man made good by the power of Christ."

Here is a man, untaught and untutored in Biblical theology. With a copy of the Bible available to him for a limited time, in his solitary confinement at a Japanese prison camp, he experiences the great illumination. The light that was in the face of Jesus Christ shines into his desperate, sinful, despairing heart.

Here is Christian love "made flesh," living in a Japanese prison. A war prisoner, victim of brutal treatment, responds with love and kindness. He turns the other cheek, loves his enemies, and prays for those who hate and persecute! This is NEWS! The modern cynic says, "Nobody ever lives this way. This is for theological discussion, but not for Main Street. It exists in Heaven, but not here!"

Jacob DeShazer's life gives the lie to all such temporizing. Such a change is unexplainable in human terms. The bombardier, with a heart of hate, is changed! Here is miracle -- hate turned to love -- living in this world! But there is more. DeShazer finds the only basis for world peace. It is a realistic approach. What Christ can do for DeShazer, He can do for the world. So DeShazer's steps are dogged by newspaper reporters, trying to discover his secret. Crowds gather to hear his simple story. Thousands repent of their sins in his services. The Associated Press estimates the number of converts at 30,000 during his first year in Japan. By his own report, 4,000 confessed and repented of their sins, and gave evidence of changed lives, in one 15-day campaign!

Here is a cool, fresh, invigorating breeze from the Eternal City, to inspire the disillusioned and strengthen the weary. God's in His world, working through DeShazer, changing men and changing the world. This is the power of the Gospel unto salvation, of which we are not ashamed!

Byron S. Lamson

Introduction

Early on the morning of December 28, 1948, the world witnessed another startling event in one of the greatest continuing miracles in modern missionary annals.

The International Press had been alerted. Representatives from the Japanese Press were waiting. Photographers were standing by. Military men, civil authorities, religious leaders, old men, young men, women, and children were at the Yokohama dock anxiously awaiting the arrival of a steamship from America.

Why all the excitement? Word had been flashed from America that the Doolittle raider who had turned missionary was to arrive on a ship that very morning.

Little did the populace know the wonderful and miraculous story connected with the modest young man, who was the center of attention as he with his wife and son came down the gangplank. But former Sergeant (now the Reverend) Jacob DeShazer knew. He knew the meaning of a Christian home; he knew how a mother's prayers can follow one; he knew the discouragement of failure, the remorse of sin, the call to daring achievement, the reproach of being captured, the pain of punishment, the meaning of a death sentence -- and a thousand other experiences.

But on this December morning, when the sky was overcast and rain was falling, DeShazer was not thinking of the many things which were in the minds of the news writers. His thoughts reached into the past, but not to recount experiences of pain and suffering. Instead, he was thinking of his debt to Christ for making it possible for him, who nearly seven years before had flown over Japan to kill and destroy, now to return with a message of love and hope.

As he viewed the throng at the dock, his thoughts quickly shifted from the past to the future. Here was Japan, once a great though pagan nation, now a defeated and disillusioned people. What poverty, what spiritual hunger! Yes, but what an opportunity!

Within a few days he was being called upon to speak to various Japanese groups. Within a few weeks he was speaking many times a day. News of the return to Japan of a man whom the Japanese had tortured in prison for more than three years gripped the popular mind. Churches, schools, factories, clubs, and other organizations were calling for him to come and tell what to them seemed an unbelievable story.

Interest in DeShazer's return to Japan has been worldwide. Seldom has there been a greater demonstration of such interest by all peoples as in this sincere and bona fide application of the principles of Christianity to peace and understanding between nations. Sermons are many and books are plentiful which extol the Golden Rule and the Sermon on the Mount, but to see these principles embodied in an actual living person was a new kind of news.

Many have been the instances, particularly during a national or world crisis, when individual men have become heroic. Great emergencies, like wars, produce leaders whose names become immortal. Not often, however, does a man reach the heights of public attention and world approbation merely by loving his enemies and acting accordingly. Herein lies the beauty and interest of the DeShazer narrative. In this regard it appeals to both the Christian and non-Christian.

But to the Christian there is far more than beauty and interest. There is a recognition and an appreciation of the hand of God. The Christian agrees that it has not been by chance that the life of DeShazer has moved along as it has.

To indicate something of the love and mercy of God in one young man's life is one purpose of this story. It is not to laud DeShazer, his parents, his college, his church, or his mission. Rather, it is to honor the Lord for His glory, to show how God intervened in answering prayer by bringing a rebellious army man to accept Christ as his Lord and Savior, and also to show how the Lord opened the way for this new convert to give himself so completely into the hands of God that he was able to carry out his prison decision to return to Japan as a messenger of God's love and grace.

It is the desire of the author that every reader of this narrative shall himself be led to a closer walk with God. DeShazer published his own life story in Japanese for the primary purpose of bringing people to Christ. In like manner he shares with the author of the English publication an equal desire that many readers will respond without reserve to the call of God in their own lives.

C.H.W.

1. A Product of the Western Frontier

Jacob DeShazer was born in Salem, Oregon, November 15, 1912. His parents were devout Christian people of modest circumstances. His father was a minister-farmer in the Church of God. He worked on the farm during the week and preached on Sunday. Within two years after Jacob's birth his father died. After three years his mother married again. Jacob's new dad was Mr. H.P. Andrus; the new home was established in a small village in north central Oregon.

The locality where anyone grows up, especially if it includes the entire period of one's childhood and youth, has a great deal to do with the development of the individual. Certainly this was true in the case of DeShazer.

He did his entire elementary and high school work in Madras, Oregon. The windswept prairie town with its population of fewer than three hundred was DeShazer's home from the time he was five years of age. Here he gained many ideas and learned something of the necessity for work, the privilege of citizenship, and the meaning of community responsibility. In school he studied history of America and the world. In Sunday school and church he came into contact with the religious forces of the community.

Starting to high school in 1927 was a great experience. Mathematics seems to have been his favorite subject. Although somewhat shy, he became active in high school athletics. He played baseball and football. On Sundays he continued to go with his family to Sunday school in the local Free Methodist Church. If he stayed for the morning preaching service, he usually disappeared quickly after the benediction, rather than stay around and meet people. During the week, aside from the time required for athletic practice, he spent most of his spare hours on the farm.

DeShazer did not openly rebel against his parents, but from time to time he did things which he knew were not right. He smoked cigarettes and occasionally played hooky from school. For a time he almost developed a habit of stealing. Fortunately, this tendency was nipped in the bud. He was caught one time red-handed after he had stolen a man's suitcase. His mother and stepfather took the matter in hand, prayed with him and for him, and then required that he make necessary apology and restitution. He reports, "It was hard to face my fine Christian parents and the neighbors after I had been reported as a thief. However, it was a very sure way to cure me of stealing."

Following his graduation from high school in 1931, DeShazer tried to get work in the community around Madras. He wanted to save money for the establishment of a home of his own. For many months he worked for one ranch neighbor, then another. Wages at that time were a dollar a day and board. It seemed that the calls for money were beyond his resources. He found it impossible to save even a portion of his wages.

After some years he heard about an opening for a camp tender for sheepherders on the California-Nevada border. He accepted the position and worked there for two years. It was healthful and vigorous work. It required, of course, that he be outdoors most of the time. He fairly lived in the saddle, for it was his responsibility to carry supplies by pack-mule train into the mountains for the sheepherders. His comment regarding this experience is, "I enjoyed going to the mountains in the summertime and back to the deserts of Nevada in the wintertime."

After two years, with little opportunity to spend money, he had accumulated one thousand dollars. With this "nest egg" in the bank, he felt that he was ready to go into business. Not wanting to go back to his hometown, he located in Butte Falls, southwest of the Crater Lake area in Oregon. He decided to raise turkeys. Having made a considerable study of turkey raising, he felt he knew both the science and art involved. Subsequent developments made it clear, however, that he did not know some of the economic problems associated with such a speculative venture. He bought five hundred day-old turkeys. Through the weeks he cared for them day and night. He watched them with great interest and anticipated their growth and development. Nothing was spared by way of providing correct food mixtures, proper shelter, and personal care.

By the holiday season his birds were in prime condition and ready for market. To his dismay, however, he found that the price of turkeys had taken a sudden drop from twenty-two cents a pound to only fourteen cents a pound. There was nothing he could do to avert financial disaster. Reluctantly he marketed his birds. When all bills were paid, not only was there no profit, but his entire one-thousand-dollar investment was gone. He had no money for a further business venture. This seems to have satisfied DeShazer's urge to go into business for himself. Once more he was confronted with the question, Where to go and what to do?

In DeShazer's early life, though not in his memory, had been World War I with all of its tragedy. During the years prior to that first world conflict, American statesmen and international experts had been saying that an international conflict was impossible. But these men and all of their followers were soon to be disillusioned when the German Kaiser mobilized his troops. During the early days of that war, Americans felt that this country was safe because the Atlantic Ocean intervened. Then, too, we had the Monroe Doctrine! In spite of ominous war clouds, the leaders thought there would be no difficulty in keeping European enemies away from the Western Hemisphere. Our position seemed quite secure.

But this sense of security was ill-founded. Soon practically the whole world was plunged into a deadly massacre, which wiped out nearly thirty million lives. An armistice came in 1918 - but it was only an armistice. The seeds for another war had already been sown.

Little more than two decades had passed when the armistice ended, and World War II broke out. Statesmen were very uneasy. America, once again, was trying to convince herself that she was safe, but at the same time the United States military leaders, hoping not to be caught unprepared as they were in 1917, called for and obtained "peace-time conscription."

DeShazer came to realize something of the situation. The United States Army was offering good pay. Then, too, he knew that as a single man he was a most eligible individual for army service in the event of war. Consequently, he enlisted. This was two years before Pearl Harbor. During this two-year period, DeShazer received basic training as an airplane mechanic and a bombardier. For a full year he was located at the McChord Field, just south of Tacoma, Washington.

2.   Army Volunteers for Secret Mission

The United States and Japan were allies during World War I. Within a few years after the armistice of 1918, however, evidences were mounting of a growing distrust and of tension between the two countries. The United States objected to Japan's aggressive policy in China. Furthermore, Japan was openly violating various international treaties. Behind the scenes, as subsequent records show, relations between the countries came almost to the breaking point several times. When World War II broke out in Europe and Japan sided with Germany, it further shook diplomatic relations . . . then came Pearl Harbor!

Overnight hatreds against Japan in this country spread throughout the entire nation and rose to a white heat. Within a few weeks the Army on the west coast moved more than one hundred thousand persons of Japanese descent to concentration camps in the interior - this, in spite of the fact that half of these were American citizens.

Our national hatred toward the Japanese was further inflamed by the information released by the State Department regarding the treachery and duplicity of the Japanese ambassador in Washington, D.C., just before Pearl Harbor.

After Pearl Harbor came Wake, Guam, Manila, and the Java Straits, and then Bataan. All of these names became fixed in the American mind, but always as defeats. The American people were wondering whether there never would come news of something besides defeat. Our Navy and Air Force had been driven back. There was a pressing demand for the military authorities to do something quickly and emphatically to jar the Japanese leaders.

So it was, the military authorities decided to make an unprecedented raid on the Japanese mainland. Perhaps our bombers could set the flimsy houses in Tokyo aflame and start a great conflagration, such as that which followed the earthquake of 1923. In any event, the chance to make such an experiment with the possibility of jarring the Japanese and at the same time increasing the confidence of the American people in their own military leaders was worth the risk.

The matter was given careful thought. Extensive investigations were made regarding individual and social reactions of the Japanese people. Finally, it was agreed to make a military raid with care not to bomb the Imperial Palace. It was planned that nothing would be bombed except military installations. To carry out such a raid meant much planning and intense training.

Army life, prior to Pearl Harbor, included much routine, much moving about, but not much excitement. Two years of this kind of life produced the same effect on DeShazer as on most other careless-minded youths. His comment on this period is no credit to him nor to the average American soldier.

> I had been living the kind of life that most of the enlisted men lived. I would associate with certain fellows and we would go to dances and drinking places to pass away our spare time. I feel ashamed of the events that took place in my life during those years. There is really no reason why anyone should want to live such a life. It does not lead to happiness.

After the bombing of Pearl Harbor, DeShazer was sent to the air base at Columbia, South Carolina. Here he was given further training as a bombardier. While he was on duty one day in this capacity, word came for him to report to his captain. In the usual sense of the term he had been a good soldier, but at the same time being reprimanded was not an unknown experience to DeShazer. On this occasion he thought probably he was scheduled for another reprimand and would be assigned again to some form of K.P. duty.

To his surprise he found some fifteen or twenty other fellows in the captain's office when he arrived. Without any preliminary statement the captain asked them whether they would like to volunteer for a dangerous mission. The whole thing was so sudden they hardly knew how to react. They began to question regarding the nature of the mission, its destination, and purpose. The captain then explained something of its danger and hazard but said it was so secret he could not tell them the details.

The more he talked, however, the more the proposition sounded to the fellows like a great adventure. Everyone who had reported to the captain's office volunteered immediately.

As a result, the whole program of DeShazer's daily life was changed and that completely. The same was true with the volunteers. Excitement ran high. Soldiers who had not volunteered looked on with a certain degree of envy. Everything about the project was so mysterious and secret that it daily gathered glamour and interest. DeShazer was glad he had been chosen. He was not able to answer the query how it happened that he was "so fortunate" - but God had a purpose!

Within a few days the volunteers for this dangerous mission were sent to Eglin Field in Florida. Here they were subjected to intensive training in all types of air maneuvers. DeShazer continued his training as airplane mechanic and bombardier. It was obvious that the secret mission would require low flying and bombing, for much time was given during this intensive training period to flying airplanes very low. DeShazer's pilot, Lieutenant William Farrow, and the other members of the crew almost made a sport of their practice. Sometimes they flew so low across fields that they had to rise to go over the fences. At other times they flew along and inside a ditch so low that the banks of the ditch were higher than the airplane itself. Experiences were many, hazards were numerous, and accidents were frequent.

General James Doolittle, at that time a lieutenant-colonel, had been placed in charge of the expedition. He went to Washington to receive special orders and special instructions. Here he was told he could have practically anything he felt necessary in order to carry out the mission successfully. His requests were to have top priority. The cost was not to be a matter of consideration. The raid itself was to be the all-important thing.

With the return of Doolittle from Washington, the training was greatly intensified. Airplanes were loaded with heavy dud bombs, and the pilots tried to get the planes off the ground by flying very short distances.

This program of training continued for a full month. Then came the order to leave Florida and go to San Francisco. The crews turned the trip across the United States into a practice flight. Most of the way they flew very low. DeShazer's comment regarding this cross-country flight suggests an initial excitement far different from that of the final raid.

> When we got to Texas and New Mexico, we could see the cattle in the fields. Our pilots would fly low in order to frighten the animals. It was great sport to see them put their tails in the air and run for all they were worth. We thought that was lots of fun and were glad to be in the Army and see something exciting.

On April 1 - April Fool's Day - 1942, the airplanes, sixteen in number, were hoisted to the flight deck of the aircraft carrier, U.S.S. *Hornet.* They were B-25 North American bombers. DeShazer's plane was the last one, No. 16. It was anchored to the flight deck with a portion of the tail assembly hanging over the stern.

The next day, April 2, the *Hornet* left San Francisco Bay and sailed out under the Golden Gate Bridge. It was high noon, and a spirit of adventure and celebration possessed everyone.

From time to time other ships joined the convoy until the entire Task Force consisted of twelve ships: the aircraft carrier *Hornet,* another aircraft carrier, the *Enterprise,* two cruisers, two tankers, and six destroyers.

They were only about ten miles offshore when the announcement blared forth over the public address system of the *Hornet* describing something of the expedition. They were told that the objective was the bombing of Japan. They were also told that they were not going to stop at another port before the bombers would be launched for the raid.

Sailors and airmen alike began to cheer. Great was the commotion. This is understandable when one remembers there were more that two thousand sailors on the *Hornet*. In addition to these were the one hundred sixty Air Corps men assigned to General Doolittle's squadron. The entire group was celebrating, not only because they were participating in a great adventure, but also because they were sharing in the feeling of many that the bombing of Japan would help to bring to a halt the awful aggression of the Japanese.

American schools are noted for their emphasis upon peace and international goodwill. Notwithstanding this, these men, although indoctrinated in the American schools to hate war, were ready to fight. Speaking of these experiences later, DeShazer says,

> I sensed a fighting spirit among these men. We did not have to have speeches to point out what was wrong with Japan. Every person seemed to know that Japan was an outlaw and would have to be forced to surrender. The Japanese were taking things that didn't belong to them. They had started the war. These American men were ready to fight against such unrighteousness.

The men felt that they were going on a real crusade. Theirs was the opportunity and the task to change the bad news of war to good news. They felt that, given the opportunity, they would be able to make a vital blow against the Japanese war machine. It seems that every fellow was thrilled with the thought of being a part of the expedition. The sailors on the *Hornet* looked on the Air Corps men with envy. It is interesting to note in this connection that the eighty airmen held in reserve in the event anyone in the first line of volunteers lost heart were all disappointed. No one became ill, and no one backed out. Thus, no replacements were made.

The pilot of DeShazer's plane, Lieutenant William Farrow, was six feet six inches tall. He was from the South. The co-pilot, Lieutenant Hites, was from Texas; the navigator, Lieutenant Barr, from New York; and the rear gunner, Sergeant Spaatz, from Kansas. The bombardier was Sergeant Jacob DeShazer, at that time a corporal. Naturally, these men became well acquainted during their period of intensive training. In those days, however, they did not realize fully how well they would become acquainted during the next three years. Speaking of their ability, DeShazer said modestly, "We found out that we were the least trained of any of the crews of the B-25's."

DeShazer had many experiences as an army man as well as in the Army Air Corps. He had frequently wondered, however, what life would be like on a ship. This was his first contact with the Navy. Even this experience on the sea amounted to little more than two weeks - but here he was, on a aircraft carrier and a member of a favored few!

On his very first night on shipboard DeShazer was called out for guard duty. About midnight when everything was dark, he apparently lost some of his courage. Even though he had a 45 pistol strapped to his side, he began to have strange feelings as he contemplated the future. He says,

> I began to wonder how many more days I was to spend in this world. Maybe I wasn't so fortunate after all to get to go on this trip. I tried to comfort myself with statistics which I could recall. I reminded myself that only 50,000 Americans had been killed in the first World War. I shuddered to think where I would go if I was to die.

During the day, however, things were different. Something of interest was happening every hour. A part of the time the airmen watched the Marines as they practiced with anti-aircraft guns on the ship. Sometimes the gunners climbed into their own airplanes and shot the guns. At times they rigged up kites for targets as they practiced shooting. Men of the Air Corps were given the privilege of going about the *Hornet* looking at the engines, the various quarters, and like.

Seals swimming alongside the ship were of great interest. The albatross, particularly, drew DeShazer's attention. In recalling these experiences he says,

> The albatross followed us, flying on tireless wings. I watched their graceful flying each day. It seemed strange that they could keep up to the aircraft carrier and never appear to move their wings. I studied aerodynamics in the army schools, but I did not understand the flying ease of the albatross. I did notice that their tail feathers acted similar to a rudder on an airplane. These strange birds didn't have to go to school to learn how to fly. They were shown the way to fly by their Creator.

In looking back over those days, DeShazer made other observations. Evidently, being out on the great Pacific Ocean, where nothing was seen for days except the blue water that seemed to be continually moving, he became meditative. He says,

> I felt a longing for something which is hard to describe. I did not know what that longing was at that time. The Creator was certainly trying to manifest himself to me by this great display of His creation. Job 12:9 tells us, "Who knoweth not in all these that the hand of the Lord hath wrought this?" I longed for fellowship with this Creator. I did not know at that time how God would gladly fellowship with His creation. I did not realize that God

would gladly fellowship with me, if I would meet the conditions written in the Bible.

One very interesting sight to all men on board the *Hornet* was the refueling of the ships from the tankers. To refuel at sea is a difficult and dangerous undertaking. One day an oil tanker pulled alongside the *Hornet* for this purpose. The sea was unusually rough. Waves of water were actually breaking over the tanker itself. Suddenly the nose of the tanker dipped down into a huge, rolling wave. When it came up riding the waves again, it was discovered that a man was overboard. He was wearing a life vest. Quickly, someone from on deck threw an inflated raft to him. The sailor seized this. Soon he was seen sitting on the raft and waving his hand at the other ships in the convoy, and the unhappy sailor was picked up by one of the destroyers. An announcement was later made over the public address system that the sailor was uninjured.

Sunday, April 5, was Easter Sunday. In keeping with the day an Easter service was held aboard the ship. Reports say it was surprising how many men showed up. DeShazer, however, was not interested. He did not attend.

The convoy kept going day after day. Included in the routine were talks by various naval officers who told about Japan, the Japanese Army and Navy, Japanese economic conditions, and the general layout. Much attention was also given to Japan's industrial setup, her water systems, fire hazards, balloon barrages, and the like. Much time, too, was spent in idleness, card playing, and shooting craps.

3.   General Quarters Alarm

Prior to Friday, April 17, the men on the ships other than the *Hornet* did not know the nature of the mission. On that day, however, the commander of the Task Force made this announcement: "This Task Force has been directed to proceed to a position four hundred miles east of Japan. The Army bombers will be launched from the U.S.S. *Hornet*. They will bomb Tokyo." Now the sailors and the men on the other eleven ships in the convoy knew the purpose of the secret trip.

When the announcement came over the loudspeakers, most of the men were seated at lunch. At first everyone seemed to be frozen to his seat. Then spirits brightened, and on some ships gay little songs were cheerfully sung. Some of these to the tune of "Snow White" went, "Hi, ho, we're off to Tokyo. We will bomb and blast and come back fast." Perhaps the cheeriness was essentially "whistling in the dark," for everywhere there was unmistakable tenseness. A strange feeling seemed to fill the air. It was evidenced on every ship, whether on the bridge, in the lookouts, in the crew's mess, or in the quarters. A question arose in the mind of each one: How close to Tokyo can we get without being spotted? This question, of course, had to go unanswered, at least for the time.

Throughout the hours of the evening and night everything was grim and silent, and yet the ships, under forced draft, were steaming ever westward. Everyone felt the zero hour was not far away. The sea was heavy, the sky was overcast, white-capped rollers flew over the tossing bows of the battleships. Spray splashed over the flight decks of the carriers. The lookouts were being soaked in the driving rain. The men in the ward room of the *Hornet* spent most of their time looking at a big map on the wall. Few words were spoken and fewer jokes. Finally, the men turned in, but most of them turned in with their clothes on.

No one knew exactly when the order would be given for Doolittle to take off. It is now known that the original plan was for them to take off late on the evening of Saturday, April 18, in order to arrive in Japan early Sunday morning and go on across to China so as to land before dark. But these plans were changed. This changed the entire outcome of the raid, particularly with respect to DeShazer and his crew mates.

The first factor which had a part in changing the plans was the sighting of two Japanese surface craft. It was believed certain they were a part of the patrol maintained by the Japanese. Immediately a General Quarters Alarm was given. This was about three-fifteen, the morning of

Saturday, April 18. A General Quarters Alarm is a piercing "Clang! Clang! Clang!" which is a call for all hands to go to battle stations. Immediately men poured up through the hatches, and in the blackness covers came off guns. Ammunition was made ready.

The alarm, of course, aroused the Army Air Corps men on the *Hornet*. DeShazer and the other Doolittle men were quickly up and waiting. In the meantime they watched the proceedings. Fortunately, the enemy ships apparently did not see the convoy, at that time nearly nine hundred miles east of Japan. It was hoped they could sail to within four hundred miles of Japan before launching the airplanes. There was constant fear, however, that some patrol boat of the Japanese might sight them.

Shortly after dawn, a Japanese fishing vessel was sighted, and low on the horizon were two Japanese ships which appeared to be destroyers. The commander of the Task Force now felt it was impossible to keep his presence unknown. He was reasonably certain that these ships had seen the convoy and of course had radioed its strength and position to Tokyo.

Suddenly one of Halsey's cruisers started shooting. This was real warfare. The big guns were booming, and it looked as though the whole side of the cruiser was on fire. Although the seas were heavy, making accurate firing difficult, the fishing boat quickly sank, one end sticking up toward the sky as it went down. Another cruiser left the convoy and took after the Japanese ships, disappearing over the horizon. After a time when the cruiser reappeared, it was announced that both enemy ships had been sunk, and although the cruiser had attempted to pick up survivors, all the men had gone down before it arrived at the scene of the wreckage.

A decision had to be made. Should the convoy attempt to go in closer to Japan, or should the bombers take off? At about eight o'clock in the morning the crisp significant order was given. The words which came over the *Hornet*'s loudspeakers stated: "Army Personnel, man your planes." This was repeated several times. Loudspeakers on the accompanying ships announced, "*Hornet* preparing to launch bombers for attack on Tokyo."

Officers, cooks, engineers, and seemingly everyone else on board, crowded the decks of the other ships, watching what was happening on the *Hornet*. On the flight deck of the *Hornet*, however, there was methodical movement. Each man, of course, was wondering whether he would have any chance at all, but there was no time to stop to figure that out. Some pleasantries were exchanged. DeShazer's pilot came by and asked him whether he knew how to row a boat. All realized with approximately eight hundred miles away from any land at all -- and that enemy land -- a boat or some other device would be necessary if they expected to live out their natural lives. Another sergeant, just as he was crawling into the rear compartment of his plane, shouted to DeShazer, "We just got one chance in a thousand of making it."

Sergeant Spaatz filled gas tanks and made last minute checkups.

DeShazer helped load bombs. Everyone was anxious to see how the airplanes would get into the air. All eyes were on General Doolittle, the first to take off. With fifteen planes behind him, he had a very short distance for his takeoff, only about four hundred and fifty feet. The shortest takeoff run at any of the practice fields had been about seven hundred feet. It looked impossible. The ship pitched and the runway tossed up and down. Men on the accompanying vessels, through the rain and motor exhaust, could dimly see Doolittle's planes poised at the takeoff position.

Doolittle knew what he was doing. His motors raced faster. The aircraft carrier cut into the waves at a speed seldom equaled in naval history. The wind almost blew a person off the deck. The airplane needed very little added speed before the air speed was enough to lift it. As the forward part of the aircraft carrier went up, the navy man gave the signal. The brakes were released. The airplane fairly jumped into the air. When the *Hornet*'s bow came down, the airplane was seen in the air. It soon rose to an altitude and leveled off, and Doolittle circled over the *Hornet* in a farewell salute. Cheers rose from the throats of those who watched.

A B-25 could take off from the deck of the *Hornet*, but there was no possible way for it to land back on the carrier. Once in the air it was necessary to stay aloft or crash into the sea.

A few minutes after General Doolittle's plane left, another plane took off, then another and another. One plane disappeared over the end of the deck. Gasps were heard from the spectators, but it came up toward the sky. Soon the sky was filled with planes -- all sixteen.

To those remaining on the *Hornet* and on the decks of the other ships it was a wonderful sight. Sixteen medium American bombers with their beautiful lines, the American insignia painted boldly on the wings and fuselages, the roar of their twin motors, gave a real sense of pride.

But Sergeant DeShazer had some real experiences in his takeoff. He with his comrades was in airplane No. 16. Because of the crowded conditions his plane was pushed to the stern of the deck, the tail actually hanging over. Just before they were ready to taxi into the takeoff position, perhaps because of the wind, the nose of the airplane rose up off the deck. The tail end went down. It looked as though the plane were about to drop into the sea. Sailors quickly tied some lines to the nose of the plane, but these broke. Nothing but courage and man power would save the plane.

Every man who could get a handhold crowded in and hung on to the front end of the airplane. DeShazer himself tried to assist. By sheer grit, stamina, and human strength the plane was held on the deck. Unfortunately, one of the sailors backed into the propeller of the airplane. Lieutenant Farrow already had his motors going at fairly high speed. One of the sailor's arms was completely cut off. DeShazer assisted others in carrying him to one side so that the plane could taxi into position for the takeoff.

Before this excitement bombs had been loaded, but since the tail end was sticking out so far, it had been impossible to load the crew's bags and other equipment. After the plane was in takeoff position, it was necessary to finish loading it. This job was most difficult because of the tremendous gale blowing across the deck. When DeShazer finally got into position in the nose of the airplane, he found that something had broken the plastic nose of the plane. Instead of being wind tight and rounded, it contained a jagged hole more than a foot in diameter just at the right of the gun mount. No one had noticed it before. No doubt it occurred when the plane had bounced around and bumped into the plane ahead of it as this forward plane was getting into position to take off.

There was little that DeShazer could do, for at that very moment the pilot was speeding his engines for takeoff. The plane shook with the terrific speed of the motors. The any man was all set to give the signal for takeoff. Admiral Halsey still had the *Hornet* headed straight into the wind. Further delay was impossible. An order had been received to push the plane overboard if it could not take off. DeShazer buckled his safety belt and tried to sit easy as the plane went down the runway. It was a perfect takeoff. The last plane, like the first circled over the *Hornet* for a farewell salute.

As this last plane started westward, DeShazer observed that the *Hornet* already had changed course. With the other vessels of the convoy it had started back home. Its job was done. The "raiders" were off.

DeShazer told the pilot over the intercommunication phone that there was a big hole in the nose of the plane. Lieutenant Farrow sent his co-pilot, Lieutenant Hite, forward to investigate. They tried putting a coat in the hole, but the wind took it away. They finally gave up. There was now nothing to do but try to reach Japan, drop their bombs, and then -- perhaps disappear forever. It was a dark hour. They knew their gas supply would be short at the very best, but now with a hole in the nose of the plane, the streamline effect of the B-25 was greatly reduced.

DeShazer's plane was one of the three planes under the immediate command of Colonel John Hilger in plane No. 14. These three planes were supposed to fly in formation until they reached Japan. Lieutenant Smith with plane No. 15 was on Colonel Hilger's right wing, and Lieutenant Farrow with plane No. 16 was on his left. Colonel Hilger, however, reports that he lost sight of Farrow soon after the takeoff when they passed through a rainstorm. Evidently the slow speed of Farrow's plane because of the broken plane nose was the reason for his failure to keep in formation.

4. Bombs Japan -- Bails Out -- Captured

Lieutenant Farrow with his crew including DeShazer left the *Hornet* at 9:20 A.M. In spite of their slow speed they reached Japan about 1:00 P.M. The trip was uneventful. Very few airplanes were seen, and these apparently did not notice the American bomber approaching. Much of the distance over open water was flown at a very low altitude, perhaps only one hundred feet.

When Japan was reached, however, they found high clouds. In order to get over the mountains, it was necessary to fly up through the clouds at an altitude of about seven thousand feet. To their surprise they found people living on these mountains. Much of the flying at this altitude was just above the treetops. The Japanese people, of course, were surprised. Apparently, they did not understand that this was an enemy airplane, for some of them waved a greeting. At one time, DeShazer noticed an old gray-bearded gentleman with a cane walking along the mountain pathway. He glanced back at the plane and threw himself flat on the ground as the plane rushed by only a few feet above him.

The target which was assigned to DeShazer's plane was not in Tokyo but Nagoya about three hundred miles south of the capital city. When they reached Nagoya, the day was beautiful and the sun was shining. DeShazer reports that it did not look much like the maps they had been shown. As they approached the first target in Nagoya, the pilot said, "Get set to drop bombs at five hundred feet. There is the first target." DeShazer, in charge of the actual bombing, looked straight ahead and saw some oil storage tanks. The plane went right over the top of the highest tank at five hundred feet. DeShazer looked down the "angle line" that, for precaution, had been substituted for a bombsight and let the incendiary bomb go. He tried to drop another bomb on another tank and then suddenly noticed that three bombs had been released instead of two. Here is DeShazer's own story.

We were making a complete turn, and I smelled smoke. I wanted to see how an oil refinery looked when it was on fire. To the left of us I saw where the first bombs had dropped. There was fire all over the tank, but it had not blown up yet. What I was smelling, however, was powder of the shells that were being shot at us instead of the bombs I had dropped. I had noticed a little black smoke cloud right in front of us and evidently the hole in the nose of our airplane allowed the smoke to come inside.

We went over a big factory-looking building and dropped the last incendiary. We skimmed along down a valley on our way to the ocean. I was getting ready to shoot. There is something about being shot at that makes you want to shoot back. I had read in the newspapers one time about a German aviator shooting at French people, and I thought it was a mean thing to do. I made up my mind while on the *Hornet* that I would not shoot at civilians. But after they shot at us, I changed my mind.

I saw a man standing in a fishing boat, waving as we came along. He thought that we were Japanese. I thought that I would show him that we weren't. I shot a few shots near him, and the poor fellow stopped waving. I wasn't a very good shot, however, and therefore no harm was done.

We flew along the coast of Japan intending to fly on the thirteenth parallel to Choo Chow Lishui, in China. We saw several of the other B-25's, but did not follow any of them. When night came, we saw dimly the coastline of China, but the fog was so thick we could not tell what part of China we were approaching.

Our navigator, Lieutenant Barr, was doing lots of paper work. He said we should be over Choo Chow Lishui. The pilot circled, calling on the radio all the time. No answer came back. The fog cleared off a little. We could see a town below but no airfield.

In the tanks we had gasoline enough for only one hour. We had to do something, and Lieutenant Farrow was anxious to save the B-25. It was a good old gas burner. With a hole in the nose it had already stayed in the air for more than thirteen hours. By flying beyond Japanese-held territory we could get to Keyon in Free China, where more gasoline was stored. We might be able to see the airfield or get a response from the Chinese radio operator. After we had flown for one hour, we saw a town. Our gasoline was nearly gone. We circled the town, calling and looking for lights from an airfield but to no avail. Finally Lieutenant Farrow said, "We gotta jump." It was 11:40 P.M. by the same time as when we left the *Hornet*. The airplane was at an altitude of three thousand feet. I watched Lieutenant Barr go first, and then I jumped.

It wasn't exactly a jump. I put my legs out, and the wind knocked them against the fuselage of the airplane so hard that I had to push against the door frame in order to get out of the opening on the lower side of the fuselage. I gave a shove and then watched the plane go over my head. I lost my hat as the wind was shrieking over me. When the plane had gone beyond me, I pulled the rip cord and was given a hard but welcome jerk as the parachute immediately opened. I watched the light go out of sight from the opening in the fuselage of the plane. Soon the sound of the motors died out. Everywhere I looked it was dark. The fog was thick around me, and I felt a strange sensation of loneliness.

I had no way of knowing that I was coming down since I could not see the ground and there was no sensation of wind since the parachute had opened. I began to wonder if I would have to sit up there all night. Suddenly I hit the earth with an awful jolt. The place where I landed was the final resting grounds of a Chinaman. I threw my arms around the mound of dirt and gave it a big hug. I was glad to be back on the ground even if it was a good long way from the U.S.A. I saw several mounds of dirt and noticed that I was on a knoll. Then I realized it was a Chinese graveyard. All around were rice fields which were under water at that time of the year. I found out later that as I was coming down in the parachute my mother was awakened from her sleep and was praying for me.

DeShazer was too stunned to realize that some of his ribs were fractured in the landing. He was able, however, to move and to walk. He shot his pistol into the air several times, but there was no response from any direction. He then cut the parachute to pieces with his knife and used a portion of the silk to protect his head from the rain. He started walking. It was difficult to find his way around the rice fields, for everywhere it was muddy and slippery.

He does not know how long he walked, but in due time he came to a little brick building which apparently had been used as a shrine by some Chinese farmer. It was beside running water and had irons to be used for burning incense. Although it was very small, he was able to clear out enough space to get in and barely have room to sit. It was a shelter from the rain. Through sheer weariness he fell asleep and did not awaken until daylight. Immediately he began to look for a road.

After walking some distance, he came to a path. As he walked along this path, he began meeting people, No one, however, seemed to be interested, and no one seemed to be excited or suspicious. This made him think that he might be in Chinese territory. From time to time he stopped a man and tried to get him to tell whether it was Japanese territory or not. Seemingly no one understood his questions, or perhaps they were unwilling to say. He finally came to a store. He went in. Here he wrote a few words on a pad, but the Chinese storekeeper could give him no information.

Once again he took to the road and walked for several hours. Finally, he came to a main road and a telephone line. This was a source of real encouragement, for it appeared he might be able to get help. The few hours of walking along Chinese farms and seeing Chinese homes gave

DeShazer his first sight of the awful living conditions of the Chinese.

> I could see inside their mud houses. Chicken, pigs, and children were wading around together in filthy mud inside the house. The people had heads about the size of a four-year-old child in America. The skin on their faces was wrinkled and old looking. I didn't expect to find anything to eat, although I was getting very hungry.

He continued walking down the main highway. In due time he came to a group of houses which obviously constituted a military base. He saw some soldier outside, washing clothes in a ditch. That was one time he wished he knew how to tell the Chinese from the Japanese. Were these soldiers friends, or were they enemies? Should he go up to them and make himself known? No, he thought best not to do so.

He walked farther down the road until he came to another house. Gathering all the courage possible, he went to this house to make inquiry. Inside he found two young soldiers playing with some Chinese children. He started talking by sign language and, of course, also used English. He used the word America, and pointed to himself. He then pointed to one of the soldiers and asked, "China or Japan?"

The soldier replied, "China." He had his misgivings. Fear seemed to take possession of him. He fixed his 45 pistol so a bullet was in the chamber and the hammer was drawn back. He knew the pistol contained seven good bullets, and he was ready to shoot it out if they were Japanese.

As he stood there, he began to feel perhaps it was better for him to leave the house and go on his way. Just as he started to back away toward the door, to his consternation he found ten soldiers, armed with bayonets, pistols, and swords, standing at the entrance. He yelled at them, "China or Japan?"

As he yelled, he was holding his hand on the pistol. Instantly, they hollered back, "China."

DeShazer says, "I didn't want to start shooting at the Chinese, so I let them come in."

The soldiers came in, succeeded in getting him to shake hands, patted him on the back, and tried to act like old-time friends. Even though it was difficult to talk to each other, they succeeded in getting him to go with them down the road to a camp. As they were walking along, they stopped for a moment, and to DeShazer's further consternation he found that a bayonet was against his back. Suddenly, guns were pointing at him from every direction. The leader of the group then reached over and took his pistol from the holster.

Finally they reached the camp. The officer who met them seemed somewhat friendly. He talked abusively to the other soldiers who came out to look at him, and they quickly disappeared into their houses like a bunch of frightened children. DeShazer was seated at a table, and a fellow began asking him questions. The questioner knew English fairly well. It was now perfectly obvious to DeShazer that the men were Japanese, not Chinese. When this fact dawned upon him, he was completely discouraged. His own description of this experience indicates that his feelings were at an even lower ebb than they were months later when he was being severely punished in prison. Nevertheless he tried to let on that he did not realize they were Japanese.

In this state of mind, he seems to have been both morose and courageous. To practically every questions which was asked, his answer was, "I don't know" or "I won't tell." In his own words he says:

> The Japanese finally found out that I wouldn't tell them anything they wanted to know. So they asked me if I wanted to eat. I told them that wasn't a bad idea. They gave me some hot cakes with apple butter. Perhaps it was not apple butter, but that is as close to it as I can describe it. The taste was different from anything that I had ever eaten. It had an oriental tang. The tea and food, however, made me feel a lot better.

He saw pictures of some high-ranking officers on the wall and asked the interpreter the names of the officers, thinking this would give him some idea for sure where he was. The interpreter mentioned several names, but they meant nothing to DeShazer. Finally, it seems that the officer in charge, thinking that DeShazer knew for certain that they were Japanese, instructed the interpreter to tell him point blank, "You are in the hands of the Japanese." Now all hope was gone, but questionings continued.

"Aren't you afraid?" asked the interpreter.

"What should I be afraid of?" he asked.

For some reason or other this question brought up the question of American slang. They had an interesting discussion regarding this subject.

A short time later he was taken to another town. He reports that in spite of all his efforts he was never able to find out the names of either of these towns. Here, however, he learned that four of his comrades had also been picked up. They met for the first time the next morning and were photographed together on the front steps of the building.

5.   Inquisition in Tokyo

DeShazer almost lost track of time. How many hours it was after he had bailed out of his plane before being placed on another plane as a prisoner he does not know. At any rate, he and his comrades were placed together in a plane similar to a D-3 transport plane and flown to another city. Evidently the distance was great, for they were in the air a good share of a day. It is now known this trip took them to Nanking, China.

In the evening they were taken off the plane and had their first experience of being in an oriental prison. The cells were made of wooden bars, placed straight up and down. The room was bare except for a wooden box for a toilet. Guards walked back and forth in front of the cell. Here someone took DeShazer's wristwatch, which he never saw again. A little later he was let into a room where a group of Japanese officers began questioning him again. Describing this experience, DeShazer says:

> One of the officers, using lots of slang, said that I had better talk. He said that these were mean people, and they would torture me until I did talk. I was still blindfolded as I had been most of the time for over twelve hours and hadn't eaten all day. I had been asked questions at every opportunity, but I would always tell them that I wouldn't talk. Sometimes they would tell me about places in America where Japan had bombed and taken possession of property; then they would come up very close to my face and open their mouths and laugh.
>
> I was then led into a room, and the blindfold was removed. A little Japanese of stocky build was standing behind a table, smoking a cigar, rubbing his hands together, and talking really fast in Japanese. Several others were in the room. The man behind the table said through the interpreter, "I am the kindest judge in all China. I want to treat you real good. Everywhere I have the reputation of being the kindest judge in all China." We sat down and the judge looked at a paper.

Then, through the interpreter, the following conversation took place:
JUDGE: How do you pronounce H-O-R-N-E-T?
DESHAZER: *Hornet.*
JUDGE: And this is the aircraft carrier you flew off to bomb Japan, isn't it?

DESHAZER: I won't talk.

JUDGE: Colonel Doolittle was your commanding officer, wasn't he?

DESHAZER: I won't talk.

The judge hit the table with his fist and yelled in Japanese. The interpreter translated the judge's words, "When you speak, look me straight in the eye!"

DeShazer says that after that when questions were asked, he looked the judge straight in the eye when he gave his answer. Evidently, he was able to look him out of countenance, for he reports the judge lowered his eyes and looked away. Finally, DeShazer was told that in Japan it was considered a great honor for the judge to cut the prisoner's head off.

At this point the judge, looking at DeShazer, said (speaking in English this time), "Tomorrow morning at sunrise I'm going to have the honor of cutting your head off." As the reader considers such an experience, knowing the sequel, it seems somewhat humorous. Certainly, it was far from humorous to DeShazer. In view of the tenseness of the situation and impending tragedy, one is amazed at DeShazer's answer. From his own account we read:

> I told him I thought it would be a great honor to me if the kindest judge in China cut my head off. The judge and others laughed for the first time, and a little later I was taken to my cell.
>
> I lay in the cell all night, blindfolded, handcuffed, without blankets. The next morning at sunrise I was led out of my cell. I had no breakfast. The blindfold was taken off, the handcuffs were removed. I looked around for the judge with his weapon of execution, but I saw a fellow with a camera, and everyone was smiling. After the picture was taken, I was loaded onto a Japanese two-motored transport. Again I was blindfolded, handcuffed, and tied with ropes. I could hear some of my companions talking, but I was not able to say anything to them. Soon after the plane took to the air, we were given some good ham sandwiches.

DeShazer was due to experience more -- much more -- of the misery of war. It was a new experience to be a captive and no longer to have freedom -- to be moved and pushed about according to the whims of the enemy.

The flight carried them for several hours over water. In due time, they were again over land, and DeShazer heard the Japanese talking excitedly and, as is sometimes their custom, drawing air through their teeth. Surreptitiously, DeShazer peeked out through his blindfold and saw Mount Fuji. By this he knew he was over Japan. A little later they landed and were taken by automobile to another prison.

Again DeShazer and his comrades were subjected to questions. It was obvious the Japanese had found some papers that told the number of airplanes and the names of the crew on each airplane. The name, *Hornet*, also, was apparently on some of the papers. Evidently someone had not destroyed all the information as everyone had been instructed by Colonel Doolittle. DeShazer and his comrades were questioned in great detail regarding the aircraft carrier and the information which had been found on these papers.

One of DeShazer's comrades, Lieutenant George Barr, was a real curiosity to the Japanese because he was six feet two inches tall and had red hair. Japanese soldiers and Japanese people came and looked at him again and again in his cell as though he were on exhibition. At times they asked him what he ate and drank in order to get that color of hair. He was the first redheaded person they had ever seen. When Lieutenant Barr was asked how he came to be there, he said that he had jumped out of an airplane, and when he hit the ground, landed on his head. He said that he couldn't remember anything since that had happened.

The unexpected and bold attempt of the American airmen to bomb Japan was a great shock to General Headquarters at Tokyo. General Sugiyama, chief of the general staff, was greatly enraged at what he called "indiscriminate" bombing and declared:

> The air raids are a matter of strategic military operation. They should come under the jurisdiction of the military staff headquarters. All the investigations and punishments in regard to the raids will be conducted by our military staff headquarters in Tokyo.

Of the sixteen raiding planes, two unfortunately entered the areas which were occupied by Japanese forces. The captured flyers of these two planes were eight in number. Five of them, including DeShazer, were first sent to Nanking, and three were sent to Shanghai. The Japanese military authorities in China promptly notified the Tokyo military headquarters regarding the capture. General Headquarters promptly issued an order to have the captured flyers sent to Tokyo for questioning. This was done.

Obviously, the Doolittle air raid had taken the Japanese military authorities off guard. It was a new experience for them; consequently there was no precedent. The question immediately arose as to whether the captured airmen should be treated as war "prisoners" or as war "criminals."

From the outset, General Sugiyama felt they were war criminals and should be executed without delay.

As a result of his order, General Shigera Sawada, the commanding officer of the 13th Japanese Army stationed at Shanghai, sent the eight men to Tokyo for trial.

Very soon it developed that there was a definite difference of opinion between the military headquarters and Japanese War Department. General Sugiyama was insisting upon the death penalty for all eight captives. General Tojo, who was the premier, felt that was too severe. Besides, Japan at the time had no law which declared the death penalty to air raiders who might be captured. In spite of Premier Tojo's apparent leniency, he quickly ordered the authorities in Japan to establish a law which would impose the death penalty in order to apply it if need be to the captured Doolittle flyers. This is one way General Tojo planned to threaten other Allied flyers if they should be captured. Such treatment was entirely different from that given to ordinary captives whose punishment - after a mock trial - was usually torture and imprisonment.

The conflict between the military leaders with respect to procedure to be followed delayed the expected trial day after day and week after week. In the meantime, however, the prisoners were called before an examining board again and again. All told there were eighteen days of such inquisition. During these days all eight men were unable to carry on conversations. The five men from DeShazer's plane knew that three men had been captured from another plane but did not know the circumstances of their landing or their capture. In the intervals between the questionings, they could hear their voices in another part of the prison.

The Japanese wanted to find out where the Americans had stored gasoline in China. On one occasion DeShazer was put on his knees and beaten severely. This brought no information. He was not an officer; consequently he had not been given such information. All he could say was that he did not know.

Some of the officers were treated even more roughly than DeShazer was. Lieutenant Nielson, navigator from the other plane, was handcuffed and his hands lifted over his head to a peg on the wall. His toes just barely touched the floor. He was stretched out that way for about eight hours. Some of the other men were stretched out on boards. Towels were placed over their faces, and water was poured over their noses and mouths. They nearly suffocated. About all DeShazer can say about it now is, "It was very painful."

In the War Crimes Court in Tokyo, a statement was made to the effect that the eight American flyers were "the unfortunate victims of war." Speaking of the various types of treatment which the flyers received during this period, Lieutenant Nielson testified at the court of Shanghai at the conclusion of the war as follows:

Q.   You state that you were kicked. Where were you kicked?
A.   My leg.
Q.   Who kicked it?
A.   A Japanese military police.
Q.   How hard did he kick it?

A. He kicked me so hard that he even left a scar.
Q. By applying this sort of treatment what did he attempt to secure?
A. They wanted to know the place from where we flew.
Q. Did you receive any ill treatment during the first night at Tokyo? If you did, what kind of treatment?
A. I was slapped on my head and face and was kicked on my leg.
Q. How were you bound?
A. My arms were bound to the back of the chair, and my legs to the chair.
Q. About how many people participated in the inquiry?
A. Three military police, one interpreter, and one recorder.
Q. Where did they kick and slap?
A. They slapped my head and face and kicked my legs so hard that the wound which was received at the Shanghai prison reopened and bled.
Q. What kind of questions were you asked?
A. The source of our flight. The question whether we bombed Tokyo during the previous week or not. A question as to our station prior to the Tokyo raid and whether we were real American soldiers.
Q. How long did the inquisition last?
A. Until four o'clock in the morning.
Q. During this period of time did they continue to mistreat you?
A. Yes. I was almost continuously beaten and kicked.
Q. During the eighteen days of inquisition were you permitted to shave or take a bath?
A. No.

This type of questioning and treatment continued for approximately two months. A memorandum found in the diary of the minister of the imperial household, Mr. Kido, dated May 21, states: "Some military leaders came into my office to discuss the punishment of the captive flyers." Obviously, the matter had been reported to the Imperial Court officials. Whether the emperor had taken a hand in the matter at this time or not, the record does not show. In any event the Japanese Army Headquarters in Tokyo finally decided to have the men tried by a court martial under the 13th Army at Shanghai.

6. Death Sentence Commuted by Hirohito

The return of the prisoners from Tokyo to Shanghai was not by airplane in a few hours as they had come over some two months before. Instead, they went first by train to Nagasaki where they stayed for a night. Throughout this train trip they were handcuffed, legcuffed, and rope tied. They had not had opportunity to bathe for sixty days. The only chance even to wash their faces was a time or two with a little tea water. Under these conditions one can imagine how they must have appeared, not having shaved during the entire two months. DeShazer says concerning this train trip, "The coal soot from the train ride made us look as though we had been living in a pig sty."

At Nagasaki they were pushed into a prison cell, the walls of which were rough, cold cement. There were a few *tatami* (straw mats) on the floor. The stench from the toilet in the corner of the little room was revolting. After a while one of the guards came and put something in the toilet to stop the awful smell. In spite of the unbearable conditions, the terrible surroundings, and the fact that they were already suffering from dysentery, the captured flyers found some joy in this prison experience at Nagasaki. For the first time since they had been captured, they were able to be together and talk with one another without interference from the guards. The five men from plane No. 16, of course, had been able to talk some together, but as yet they did not know the story concerning the three other men.

DeShazer admits they almost forgot the filth and dirt while he and his four comrades from plane No. 16 listened to the thrilling story of the three men from plane No. 6. The pilot of plane No. 6 was Lieutenant Dean Hallmark from Texas; the co-pilot, Lieutenant Robert Meder from Ohio; the navigator, Lieutenant C. T. Nielson. The bombardier and the rear gunner had been lost in the crash landing at sea. Here is the story:

The plane ran out of gas just as it reached the China coast. Lieutenant Hallmark tried to gain altitude and fly over the mountains, but the airplane engine finally sputtered and died. They made a crash landing in the ocean and then found that their rubber life raft was no good. Thinking that the plane would sink immediately, all five men jumped into the water and started for the shore.

The bombardier and the rear gunner seemed to be having trouble. Lieutenant Meder came back and tried to help the rear gunner. Lieutenant Hallmark and Lieutenant Nielson were not aware that any of the men were

30

having difficulty. The water was icy cold and they were far from shore.

Lieutenant Meder was a true soldier and a courageous soul. He did his best to help the rear gunner, who evidently had been injured in the crash landing. With almost unbelievable courage and endurance, Lieutenant Meder held on to his mate and swam in the icy water until dawn. It seemed that Meder could not let go although his comrade had become entirely unconscious. His frame was entirely limp. Undoubtedly, he was lifeless. Lieutenant Meder was finally able to reach the shore with the body of his friend. Meder was completely exhausted. He collapsed on the beach, hardly out of reach of the water. In time, however, he revived somewhat and gained enough strength to climb farther up the beach. There to his amazement he saw the body of the bombardier lying on the sand. The tide had already brought him to shore faster than Meder himself had been able to swim with the limp form of the gunner. With all the strength he could gather, he tried his best to revive both men, but it was too late.

Thus there were only three survivors of plane No. 6. The men were not together when they reached the beach. Each one had to follow his best judgement. When Lieutenant Nielson reached the beach, he tried to crawl up the bank and seek some shelter and warmth. Suddenly, he felt himself falling. When he came to, it was daylight. He had fallen into a small canyon. He soon found a path and followed this until he came to a small village.

Lieutenant Hallmark had remained on the beach until daylight and then began looking around to get his bearings. He, too, found a path and walked into a village. To see an American soldier was an unusual sight, and he was quickly surrounded by Chinese soldiers. They took him to a small mud house and gave him some tea. Some of the Chinese tried to talk to him, but he could not understand them. Finally, one of the Chinese indicated that someone was coming. Lieutenant Hallmark thought that the Chinese were trying to warn him that the Japanese were coming to capture him. He picked up a large club and stood by the door with the club over his head. The door opened, and Lieutenant Nielson walked into the room. What a meeting! Although only a few hours' time had elapsed since they had been together, the experiences through which they had gone made it seem as if days had passed.

In due time, Lieutenant Meder was discovered by the Chinese, and all three were brought together. The Chinese seemed to be gracious and gave them food. Referring to their description of this experience at a later time, DeShazer says:

> It must have been fairly good food, for many times when hunger pangs were upon us, months later, we would hear these three refer to the food which they had eaten on this occasion.

The Chinese soldiers acted as if they were going to help the airmen evade the Japanese. Great was their disappointment when these very Chinese soldiers turned them over to Japanese officials. They were taken to Shanghai and later flown to Tokyo. Then all eight were together in the same prison cell at Nagasaki.

To their great relief, they spent but one night in this awful prison. The surroundings were almost unendurable. They were sick in body; yet to their real satisfaction they had opportunity to talk together. Obviously, there had been little sleep. The next morning they were put on a ship which took them, still handcuffed and tied, back to Shanghai. They arrived on June 19, 1942. The previous sixty days had been like a nightmare, but the next seventy days were to be days of stark horror.

As soon as the captives landed in Shanghai, they were taken immediately to the "Bridge House." They were in poor physical condition, greatly emaciated and barely able to move.

They were placed in a prison cell with fifteen Chinese prisoners, two of whom were women. The size of the cell was twelve by fifteen feet. An open box was used as receptacle.

Food consisted of a cup of boiled rice soup for breakfast, four ounces of bread for lunch, and four ounces of bread again for dinner. Approximately two quarts of water were given each day to the eight Americans. Lieutenant Hallmark was on a stretcher, but the other seven men, though considerably weakened, were able to stand.

Most of the other prisoners were covered with scabs and old sores. They were very weak and made a most pitiful appearance. The room was so small there was not enough space for all to lie down at one time. Bedbugs, lice, and large rats were plentiful. It was then midsummer of 1942. The weather was hot and the water available was inadequate. DeShazer in telling about the situation makes rather revealing and philosophical observations:

> One day one of the Chinese women fell down and hurt her head. They laughed and said she was pretending to be sick. Guards hit her on the head with a stick, which was attached to their keys. They seemed to be the very lowest type of people. Sometimes they would make us stand up during the night after they had awakened us from our sleep. They would threaten to hit us with long clubs which they poked through the bars of the cell.
>
> It was the first time that I had ever been in such a wicked environment. I could not help wondering why there was so much difference between America and the Orient. There is bad in America, but the bad in America does not begin to compare with that which we observed. The truth was beginning to dawn upon me -- it is Christianity that makes the difference. Even though many

people in America do not profess to be Christians, yet they are following the Christian ways. Even the non-Christian people in America do not hit women over the head. The people who are Christians have shown the rest of the world the right way to act. It is because God has said Christians are to be the light of the world. I had always tried to steer away from religion, but now I was beginning to see that Christianity is a great benefit to mankind. It is God's plan for mankind's happiness.

In the daytime we were supposed to sit straight up on the floor without any support for our backs. Often the guards would catch us leaning back on our elbows. There was always a quarrel as soon as we were caught. The guard would try to hit us on the head with a bamboo stick. The Chinese prisoners would allow themselves to be beaten and would then thank the Japanese guards. We always tried to talk the guards out of the notion of hitting us, but sometimes we would have to take the punishment.

One day the guard caught Lieutenant Hite and Lieutenant Farrow leaning against the wall. He hollered, "*Kurah*" (Hey!) and opened the door. His sword and steel scabbard were used to hit them on the head. Lieutenant Hite grabbed the weapon, and the guard pulled his sword out of the scabbard. It looked as if Hite was going to be killed, but the guard finally calmed down and acted more human.

We weren't getting much food. Lieutenant Hallmark was a large man. His frame needed something to fill it up. We were all weak from the lack of water and food. One day Lieutenant Hallmark passed out. He was very sick after that. We had to carry him to the toilet. He had dysentery, and we had to take him about every fifteen minutes. We had regular shifts, but it was too hard on us; finally, all of us gave out. We were all lying flat on our backs from exhaustion and practically ready to give up.

Such was the situation and the condition under which these American boys lived for seventy long days. Along with the sickness, filth, and constant brutality was the ever-present suspense regarding what the Japanese government was going to do with them. Rumors were frequent that they were to be executed. From time to time they were subjected to further questionings. Whatever remained of morale was scarcely perceptible. They were dejected, discouraged, and almost hopeless.

At one period during those dark days they were taken before Major-General Shoji Ito, chief justice officer of the Japanese 13th Army Military Court at Shanghai. The trial took place at the tribunal courthouse, headed by a prosecutor, Major Itsura Hata. The judges were Yamitsu, Okada, and Tatsuta. Lieutenant Hallmark had to be carried to the court on a stretcher, but the rest of the defendants stood during the trial.

There was no defense attorney, nor was there any statement declaring innocence or guilt. There was no witness. The trial could scarcely be called one of justice, for the Tokyo Headquarters had already decided the fate of the prisoners. Personal word was brought from Tokyo to Colonel Arisue. He reported that General Sugiyama expected the death penalty for each member of the group.

During the trial the prosecutor, Hata, gave the names of the eight prisoners and then proceeded to state the evidences of the "indiscriminate bombings" during the Doolittle raid over Japanese cities. He reported that in these raids nonmilitary people had been killed. He also declared that the bombings were against the military laws; therefore, all of the flyers who participated in this offense would receive the death sentence.

At the conclusion of the trial, the judges condemned all eight of the Americans to be executed. The verdict was promptly relayed to Tokyo. The American airmen, of course, were not informed.

General Sugiyama thought the death sentence was proper. There were many, however, in the department of the Japanese Army and in the army of occupation of Shanghai, who felt that the punishment was stricter than necessary. This idea was undoubtedly due to the fact that the war had just begun and the people as yet were not as war-minded as later on. At that time the punishment seemed too severe. The people's attitude in this regard toward the end of the war would certainly have been different, for by that time hatred against the victorious Americans had mounted. Many weeks passed by as the matter was being given final consideration at the Tokyo Headquarters.

In the meantime conditions in the prison at the "Bridge House" and the health of the prisoners had reached the point where it was absolutely necessary to improve the situation if the prisoners were to continue to live at all. So it was that after they had spent seventy days in the twelve-by-fifteen cell, the prisoners were taken out and moved to another prison just outside Shanghai. Lieutenant Hallmark was wrapped in a blanket and laid on the floor. Again they were all taken before some Japanese Army officials to answer questions and tell about their past history.

In this new prison solitary confinement began in earnest. Each man was placed in a small cell about nine-by-five feet. The conditions were materially better than in the previous prison, but at the same time there was still the haunting fear, both throughout the day and during the long nights, that at any time they might be called out to face a firing squad or something worse.

During these days among the Tokyo officials some interesting things were happening. Jealousies and rivalries between top army leaders and officials in the War Cabinet flared up and played a part in the final decision regarding the sentence of death on the American flyers. According to the records, it is now known that the incident had been reported to the Imperial Court family. The record of the minister of the imperial household states that on October 3, 1942,

> Premier Tojo came in at 11:30. He gave a detailed account of the capture of the flyers and the proposed punishment. I was requested to report it to the emperor. I was given an audience by the emperor from 1:05 to 1:15 P.M., and related Tojo's message to him.

The record further shows that Kido, the minister of the Imperial Household, told the emperor that Tojo was in favor of a more lenient punishment but that a formal decision of the death penalty for all the flyers had been made by a responsible authority, General Sugiyama, chief of the general staff.

In the international Military Tribunal which was held in Tokyo following the close of the war, testimony was given which shows that there was considerable rivalry between General Sugiyama and General Tojo in this connection. It seems that each general was trying to get an audience with the emperor in advance of the other. If General Sugiyama[1] had been able to have talked with the emperor first, undoubtedly all the prisoners would have been executed. Tojo, however, was able to reach the emperor first and make a request for leniency before Sugiyama had made a formal demand for the death penalty. Sugiyama continued his insistence that the Americans were criminals.

Some of the questions and answers which appear on the record of the International Military Tribunal regarding this matter, though somewhat difficult to understand, will be of interest. The questions were put to General Tojo[2] by an Allied prosecutor:

Q.   When General Sugiyama requested the death sentence for the flyers, did he come to you as a representative of someone in the Imperial Headquarters?

A.   No. He did not represent anyone. He came along on his own initiative. Since the chief of the general staff had seldom shown up by himself, I can remember the incident very well.

Q.   Have you ever discussed this order with the emperor?

---

[1] Sugiyama committed suicide on the day Japan surrendered.

[2] General Tojo was executed by the Allied military authorities following this trial.

A.   No. The emperor did not enter into this matter. The reports from the court-martial which took place in China showed that General Sugiyama had asked for a verdict of death for all eight flyers. The chief of the general staff came to me demanding that the decision be carried out without failure. However, since I had known of the humane nature of the emperor, it would be to his wish that the death penalty be applied to the smallest possible number of prisoners. For this reason only the three who had killed a schoolchild were to receive the death sentence. I consulted the emperor regarding this matter, for he was the only authority who could issue the reduction of the sentence. This is the only point which was called to the emperor's attention.

Q.   In other words the emperor reexamined the issue and reduced the death penalty of the eight flyers to three, did he not?

A.   No. He did not reexamine the issue. In Japan the decision made by the court-martial cannot be reexamined and changed.

Q.   What made the emperor decide this way? Was it because of your suggestions?

A.   Yes. His advisers usually discussed issues of importance with him. However, it was the emperor who reduced the sentence. He was very generous.

Q.   After a long discussion of the verdict, Sugiyama went to the palace and was informed that the emperor had commuted the sentence. Thereupon, Sugiyama wired General Hata, commanding general in occupied China, as follows: "I believe the verdict issued by the chief prosecutor at the military tribunal was fair. However, I am convinced that the sentence for the flyers should be commuted, except for three flyers. The others will receive life sentences. Lieutenant Colonel Takayama will be dispatched from Fukukoka on the fourteenth of this month (October) to carry out the punishment. All questions should be directed to him."

A further message was sent from General Sugiyama listing the names of the flyers sentenced to death: Pilot Hallmark, Pilot Farrow, and machine gunner Spaatz; those commuted to life sentences: Meder, Nielson, Hite, Barr, DeShazer. This message further revealed that the death sentence was to be carried out October 15. The record does not show whether the executions were carried out on this particular date or not. The testimony in the Allied War Trials indicates that it was about that date when the three unfortunate Americans were shot, either in the outskirts of Shanghai or in a military prison yard late at night in secrecy.

Those who were condemned to life imprisonment were deprived of the privilege of prisoner's exchange. From that time on, they were not given the normal treatment received by other prisoners of war.

Of course, these military conferences and discussion were going on, wholly unknown to the American flyers. About the middle of October, when for some time they had been in solitary confinement in individual cells and yet able to be with each other a few minutes each day, suddenly they found that three of the men did not appear. From that time on, they were seen no more. The other five did not know what had happened to the three until they gained their freedom after the close of the war.

Soon after the disappearance of three of the men, the remaining five were taken into a courtroom. Knowing that three of their companions had disappeared, they were naturally worried concerning this particular move. While they were standing before the judge, he read off a long statement in Japanese. When it was interpreted, they learned that they were to receive life imprisonment with "special treatment." They were told that they had been sentenced to be executed but that the emperor of Japan had changed the order and they were to receive life imprisonment. Following this statement they were taken back to their cells - to ponder and ponder and ponder! Speaking concerning this particular experience, DeShazer says:

> I had expected to be executed from the way the Japanese had acted. It was really a relief to know that they were now planning to let us remain alive. I could not help feeling a strange sense of joy, even though solitary confinement and a long war awaited any possible chance of freedom. At the same time it seemed almost hopeless to think of ever being free again, since the most probable thing would be that we would be executed when America did win the war.

7.   Solitary Confinement

DeShazer and his four companions, not knowing what happened to their three comrades but realizing they themselves had escaped execution for the time being at least, began to think more of their immediate future. It was now just six months since they had taken off the *Hornet* amidst the cheers of thousands of American soldiers and sailors. During the six-month period they had come to know something of suffering, fear, and almost death.

Now as they looked to the future with the thought of solitary confinement and perhaps a long war, a spirit of hopelessness again took possession of them. Each was in a little cell nine-by-five feet with no windows except a small opening near the ceiling. Guards were in front of the door. There were no books, no radios, no newspapers, no play, no fellowship. Since their sentence included "special treatment" it meant no letters to or from home and no Red Cross packages. In this regard the situation was entirely different from that of an internment camp.

They remembered something of what the hot summer of 1942 had been. Now it was late October, and winter was not far away. If they had known at the time there would be no heat in the prison, even during the coldest, freezing winter weather, their spirits would have dropped even lower if that could have been possible.

As the days came and went, however, sheer necessity required that they adjust to the situation. They tried their best to fraternize with the guards. They were particularly anxious to find out what had happened to their three companions. For a few minutes each morning, they were allowed to get out of their cells in order to wash their hands and brush their teeth. Occasionally, a guard or an official would come and take them out for a little exercise.

One morning when they were taking exercises under the direction of the head official, Lieutenant Hite asked this man what had happened to the three men who had been taken to another prison camp. In the further conversation the interpreter got his words mixed and for a moment had the men aghast. The interpreter, who was really trying to befriend the Americans, told then that "they were going to all be executed." Under the shock of this statement, their faces showed how startled they were, and they also demonstrated their interest in looking for ways and means of escaping from the prison. Upon realizing his error, the interpreter said he was sorry and explained he had made a mistake. What he was trying to say was that there were to have been executed but had been granted mercy by the emperor. This statement further confirmed them in their belief that the announcement of the Japanese judge was correct in regard to their sentence to be executed having been commuted to life imprisonment. For many weeks this interpreter was a source of encouragement. He was half Japanese and half Portuguese.

The many weary hours spent in solitary confinement made it difficult to think normally. There was the constant problem of how to occupy their minds. By yelling they could hear one another from one cell to another. Yelling, however, attracted the guards and brought reprimand and punishment. At one time during a period of six or eight weeks they made somewhat of a game of their meager food rations. They worked out a little scheme of drawing numbers so one day a week the fellow who drew the winning number would receive from each of the others an extra half bowl of rice or a bowl of soup. Lieutenant Meder seems to have been the instigator of the idea. By a mere coincidence it seems that he lost more than anyone else. DeShazer rather boasted of the fact that he seemed to win more times than any of the others. Commenting on this, DeShazer says:

> We had lots of fun over this game, although it only lasted for about two months and even then only once a week. We often used to agree in advance to trade a bowl of rice for two bowls of soup. When the food came, however, we would howl and complain about the other fellow being a sharp trader if we thought he got the best of the deal. We never knew, of course, in advance what the food was going to be, but it kept us amused to trade around with one another.

It seems that throughout the rest of their imprisonment, DeShazer had fun poked at him from time to time for having been such a winner in this period of trading food.

Another activity engaged in by DeShazer in order to occupy his time was climbing the walls of his cell. Since the cell was only five feet wide, it was possible for him to put his hands on one wall and his feet on the other. By proper maneuvering he was able to climb in this fashion to the ceiling. It was about a twelve-foot climb. When up near the ceiling, he could look out the little window and see the countryside for miles around. Obviously, this was good exercise, and it was a real joy to look out on the scenery after the long hours of looking at four walls. Fortunately for him he was never caught in this act by any guard.

When winter came, DeShazer and his comrades were given some additional clothing, but still there was much suffering. Lieutenant Hite became sick and suffered from the damp, cold cell. He was very sick for about three months. During this period he became erratic, both in his conversation and in his actions. He did not return to normal until early spring.

In April 1943, practically one year after the fateful day of the Tokyo raid, DeShazer and his comrades were taken by airplane from Shanghai to Nanking. Such a move naturally aroused anticipation and a certain amount of excitement. They were particularly hoping for a nice courtyard outside the prison in which they would be free to move around. They felt that they had had their full share of solitary confinement. There was a perpetual dread in their minds of being all alone in a prison cell. There was also the dread of intense cold in the winter and extreme heat in the summer. But their hopes for relief were doomed to disappointment.

Immediately upon arriving in Nanking, they were again placed in solitary confinement. They did, however, find some relief in that occasionally the guards in the Nanking prison showed some friendship. Evidently, being a guard in a prison was itself a somewhat lonesome business. These guards, even though ordered not to give out information, did occasionally try to talk to the prisoners. It was through these conversations that the American boys were able to glean, from time to time, some scant information concerning what was going on in the war. By piecing together bits of such information they finally determined that the whole Japanese Navy had been sunk. At other times the guards would become abusive and cruel.

Each day for a few minutes DeShazer and his comrades were taken outside so their cells could be cleaned and also so the men could have a little exercise. It was during these brief moments of exercise that all five occasionally could get together. The guards would allow them to say "Hello" to one another, but if they said much more the guards would usually yell, "Shut up!"

Hours were many and long. Days were long. Week after week came and went. The hot summer of 1943 finally passed and once again there was the comfort of fall.

Occasionally, things became a little brighter. Once in a while, a guard would allow the airmen during the exercise period to talk at length among themselves. At times the guards would themselves wrestle with the prisoners. They called it *smoe*. The American men were considerably larger than their guards. In view of this the guards could not hold them down, but they were exceptionally good at kicking and tripping. Usually by this method they would finally get the Americans down. When this occurred, they immediately waved their handkerchiefs over their heads, said the match was over, and shouted, *"Nippon benzai! Nippon benzai!"* (Japan wins! Japan wins!)

The conversation of the guards concerning the war, in general, however, implied that Japan was winning all the time. Frequently they told the Americans that there was no hope for them, that everything was going in Japan's favor. As a rule, during such a conversation, they would finally swing around and say, "Well, if Japan should lose and America should win, prisoners would not be set free. Instead, they would all have their heads cut off." They insisted that the Japanese expected to fight until the last man died, and of course, they said the emperor of Japan would be the last one to die. Not once was a critical word spoken against the emperor.

Through such conversations DeShazer and his comrades came to know more of the Japanese worship of their emperor. The Japanese people believed the emperor was the representative on earth of deity. They also believed their emperor could not be wrong in any of his words or deeds. Since the emperor had asked them to fight for their country, it was their highest honor and joy to do so and, if need be, to die. Referring to some of these conversations and particularly the slant the Japanese had concerning the war, DeShazer says:

> They would tell us many fantastic tales of how God was on their side and how they were able to sink many ships with just one airplane. It seemed to be their belief that they were in the right as far as the war was concerned. They said that America had started the war. We were greatly surprised when they brought out some of their arguments. It seemed hard to understand how grown men could believe some of the things the Japanese government was telling their people. However, these men were convinced that they were in the right and that their country was going to win. They had confidence in a supernatural power that was unshakable. These bloody Chinese head-removers said that they were in the right and that God was always on the side of righteousness.

Moralizing on the situation, DeShazer says further:

> These men had never been taught about the true God. How could they know that the God who has been revealed for all mankind is on the side of peace? They did not know about Jesus who died on the cross to pay the penalty for the sin of hatred and the lust for power. They did not know about the Spirit of Jesus that will enter into a person and take away the hatred and greed of this world. They had only been taught about a god who was seeking everything for Japan. They needed to know about Jesus who was God's true representative for every nation and every generation of men.

Just about the time of the fall equinox in 1943, Lieutenant Meder took very sick with dysentery. His comrades had noticed for some time that he was looking increasingly thin and weak. One day all five were in the yard together. It was a beautiful fall day, and they were allowed to run about a little. Lieutenant Meder was able to be out but was not able to exercise. Those who were able to run around the yard together naturally would whisper to one another and exchange information concerning what they had been able to pry out of the guards. They were always very solicitous concerning each other's opinions as to how each felt. There was always the constant fear of disease taking hold of them or of their losing their mental faculties.

On this particular day they were all anxious about Meder, but they did not dare to stop and gather around him and make inquiry. Lieutenant Nielson, however, went to Meder and asked him how he was feeling. Several guards were in the yard, but one particular guard seemed to have charge of the exercise for this day. When this guard saw Nielson over at the side of the yard talking to Meder, he yelled to him, "Shut up!" Nielson paid no attention to the guard; this seemed to make him very angry. For a time the guard muttered and swore. DeShazer and the other airmen were soon required to stop running around, pick up the pails and tools which they had been using to clean the cells, and return to their cells. Once again the guard yelled at Nielson and Meder who were making the most of their time together by talking as fast as they could. Neither of the officers for a time paid any attention to the guard. When Nielson finally came up to where the guard was standing, the guard reached out and slapped Nielson's face. Lieutenant Nielson calmly set his bucket down on the ground. He cleared his throat - "Ahem." Then, slowly, without any trace of anger, Nielson reached out and slapped the guard's face.

Everyone was shocked. No one knew what happened next. Seven or eight guards had come into the yard to watch the men exercise. They all sucked air through their teeth as the Japanese do when they see something which surprises them. The guard who was slapped was humiliated and, of course, very angry. He started to strike Nielson with his steel scabbard, but Nielson was an expert in getting out of the way. DeShazer says:

> It was comical to see the way Nielson dodged the blows of the angry guard. One swing would have killed him if the guard could have made contact. One of the guards who had been watching tried to stop the fight and was rewarded for his good intentions by the swinging scabbard hitting the back of his hand. After that the fight ended.

All the men were then put back into their cells. Nielson, of course, as well as the others wondered what the penalty would be. Prisoners held by the Japanese had been beheaded for no greater breach than that which had been committed by Nielson. To the surprise of everyone, however, the whole affair was never mentioned again. It seems that most of the guards even admired Nielson for his courage.

Weeks went by. Lieutenant Meder continued to grow worse and died December 1. No one will ever know all the thoughts of this man who had spent many lonely hours suffering in that far-off prison cell. His comrades fain would have helped him, but this, of course, was out of the question. He held the highest esteem of his comrades. It was Meder who had tried to rescue two of his comrades after the crash landing at the close of that fateful day after leaving the aircraft carrier, *Hornet*. In speaking of him DeShazer says:

> Lieutenant Meder seemed to understand the Bible message well. He and I had a good talk one day while we were pulling weeds out in the yard. Meder told me that Jesus Christ is the Lord and coming King, that Jesus is God's Son and that God expects the nations and people to recognize Jesus as Lord and Savior. He said that the war would last until Jesus Christ caused it to stop. I did not understand what he meant at the time, but I remembered his words later. Lieutenant Meder had a very brilliant mind. He was truly a gentleman in every way, and he was a prince of a fellow.

Meder's comrades, however, did not know immediately of his death. Suddenly they were aware of considerable hammering out in the yard. DeShazer crawled up and peeked out the window. He saw they were making a large box. The next day DeShazer and the other three airmen, one at a time, were taken from their cells around into Meder's cell where they could take a last look. He was lying in the box with a nice wreath of flowers and a copy of the Bible on the lid of the box. A short time after, when they were back in their cells, they could tell by the sounds that the box with their comrade's body was being carried out. Later a small box was brought back, which the guard said contained the ashes of Lieutenant Meder.

Evidently the death of Lieutenant Meder, when reported to the "higher ups" in the military government in Japan, brought about reprimands and a change in procedure. In a few days the captain of the prison came in to talk to the prisoners and to try to cheer them. He even went so far as to ask what they would like to have. They responded immediately that they would like to have some bread, butter, jam, steak, eggs, milk, and other American food. They knew, of course, that no Japanese official could provide such food, but almost twenty months on rations in an oriental prison made them have an indescribable longing for American food.

To their delight the Japanese officials did arrange for them to be given bread with their ration of rice and soup. He also made arrangements for them to be fed three times, rather than twice each day. This was one of the most outstanding events during the winter of 1943-44. Soon both their health and their spirits greatly improved.

The airmen had also hoped in this new arrangement to have a change in conditions so that they could hear from home. There had been no word from America. This continued to be denied. But they were provided with a few books to read. How fortunate it was that among these books was a Bible - an American Standard Edition. DeShazer was the only man in the group who was not an officer. This meant that the other three men, being officers, had first choice with respect to reading. Not until the beginning of summer did DeShazer have the privilege of having the Bible. Even then it was his privilege for only three weeks.

Prior to the time DeShazer obtained the Bible he had the great pleasure of getting one or two other books. He made use of his time in memorizing portions from these books as indicated in a letter to the author by Captain C. J. Nielson. In describing the long weary hours in solitary confinement Nielson referred to the "gnawing hunger in [their] heads and stomachs." He indicates that each of the men resorted to different things in an effort to occupy his mind. He says:

> During those many hours and months I tried by mental pictures to plan a home. Lieutenant Barr was working on an elaborate neon sign, and Lieutenant Hite tried to plan a model farm. Meanwhile DeShazer was memorizing a very long poem, "The Pleasures of Hope," from one of the few books we were able to have. He would recite parts of it to us when we came together for our recreational period and we all learned various portions. Some of these lines will stay with me forever, such as
> "Lo, Nature, Life and Liberty illume
> The dim-eyed tenant of the dungeon gloom.
> Truth shall pervade the unfathomed darkness there.
> And light the dreadful features of despair."

8.   Three Weeks with the Bible

Only eternity will reveal exactly what happened in a little prison cell in far-off Nanking, China, sometime in May 1944. The exact day is not known, but a most significant event took place. There sat DeShazer in solitary confinement hour after hour, day after day. He was homesick, hungry, discouraged, and almost hopeless. Throughout the dreary weeks of more than two long years, he had been waiting, waiting - and thinking. Recreation had been meager. The privilege of reading was almost unknown. His comrades, however, had been telling him about the copy of the Bible which they had been reading. Then one day it came his turn.

The Bible - that was the Book he had heard read at the family altar in that little rural home just outside Madras, Oregon, years before. That was the Book from which lessons had been studied in the Sunday school in the modest little Free Methodist Church and the Methodist Episcopal Church in that same isolated village. That was the Book he had long since lost interest in - if, in truth, he had ever had interest in it - until after many months in prison.

Now it was his turn to have the Bible. It was laid in his hands. Who brought it to the prison he will never know - whether Protestant or Catholic, it does not matter. With almost feverish grasp he seized the Bible and pressed it to his bosom.

Yes, the Bible, the very Word of God! The Book of books which has been the inspiration of the lives of multiplied thousands. From the cultural and aesthetic point of view the Bible has been the inspiration of poets, artists, musicians, orators, sculptors, authors, and many others throughout the centuries. Then, too, it has been the silent inspiration of millions of people entirely lost in the masses but devout followers of Jesus Christ who have pored over its pages and received personal encouragement, comfort, and strength. This was the Book which fell into DeShazer's hands. Yes, the "best seller" according to the record of the publishers, but in a cold dingy prison cell, unknown to the most of the world, the Bible became the best-read Book to this young man.

The light in DeShazer's cell was horribly dim, and the print was fairly small, but that did not matter. He opened the Book and began to read. From then on, there was little time to sleep. He had been warned that he could have the Book only three weeks. He read and read and read! He read the entire Book through several times. He read the Prophets through six times. Many hours were spent in memorizing. The entire Bible seemed to become alive. It appeared to be illuminated. Certain passages seemed to blaze forth with mysterious brightness. Certainly, here was evidence of a profound truth, "The Word has power." We also see clear evidence of the faithful working of the Holy Spirit. DeShazer had no one to guide him, such as a pastor, a Sunday school worker, a teacher, or a friend. But the Comforter, who was sent into the world to guide into all truth, was present to guide the spiritually hungry young man.

As DeShazer continued to read his Bible and study, new truths seemed to be staring at him. Increasingly he began looking for proof of the existence of God and His revelation to human beings. As he was reading Isaiah, for instance, and thinking about the time which was hundreds of years before Christ, he came to this verse: "Surely he hath borne our griefs, and carried our sorrows: yet we did esteem him stricken, smitten of God, and afflicted. But he was wounded for our transgressions, he was bruised for our iniquities: the chastisement of our peace was upon him; and with his stripes we are healed. All we like sheep have gone astray; we have turned every one to his own way; and the Lord hath laid on him the iniquity of us all" (Isaiah 53:4-6).

DeShazer began to see how the prophecies in the Old Testament were revealed in the New. He became enamored with the sense of the supernatural. Having read the prophecy in Isaiah, he says he was greatly impressed when he came to the twenty-seventh chapter of Matthew and read how the people seeing Jesus on the cross, as Isaiah had prophesied, "esteemed him stricken, smitten of God and afflicted." They "reviled him, wagging their heads." They said, "He trusted in God; let him deliver him now, if he will have him: for he said, I am the Son of God" (Matthew 27:43). DeShazer seemed to put himself in the place of the Jews, and he felt he could understand Jesus' hanging on the cross was pure proof that Jesus was indeed a fraud. From their point of view, God had forsaken the Christ and was using this means of punishing Him. Then DeShazer, following the Gospel story, realized how the resurrection of Jesus was a complete fulfillment of the prophecy which was found in the Old Testament.

The prophets had foretold what would take place. Daniel said, "Messiah shall be cut off" (Daniel 9:26). In Zechariah 13:7 DeShazer read, "Smite the shepherd, and the sheep shall be scattered."

The perfect agreement between the writers of the Old Testament and the New was a revelation to this new student of the Bible. He was thinking:

> Yes, Christ died for us; that is the message all the way through the Bible. Many different people were writing, but the same revelation of salvation was given to every one. The same thread of thought is carried from Genesis to Revelation. I've seen proof of it in my lifetime. I've seen the handiwork of God. God has manifested himself for us to see.

Along the same line he seemed to be charmed by the love of God:

Jesus existed as God's Son before the world was created, but when the time was fulfilled God sent His Son into the world to take on the form of a human being. It was nearly two thousand years ago that this great event happened. God had foretold this event through prophecy. Now God gave the sign of miracles which Jesus performed. Jesus also claimed to be the One who fulfilled prophecy. Now God, to make sure that we could believe, raised Jesus from the dead. Jesus had died for us. We do not need to suffer the penalty for sin now. We do not need to die.

It is difficult for us in normal situations to grasp what was going on in the soul of this American prisoner as he tried to grasp the truth of the great Book. Over and over he would go back to the prophet and then come again to the New Testament. Hour after hour he read. One reference after another was followed through. Without doubt a miracle was taking place daily within his heart and mind. New insights were revealed.

The light was shining brighter and brighter. Perhaps the memory of boyhood days in Sunday school, long covered by the debris of careless thinking and worldly living, was being revived, and truths long forgotten were returning to mind. We do not know. Certainly, the Spirit of God was making it possible for DeShazer - without the assistance of priest, minister, teacher, or friend - to get a theological course unprecedented in its scope and intensity. Certainly he was coming near to the inner revelation of God to himself.

As DeShazer eagerly read the Bible, particularly the promises in the Bible, he was more and more brought to the point where he felt the message of the gospel was for him as an individual. He came to believe that all of these things were written and all of these events took place so that he could know that he had eternal life if he believed on Jesus Christ.

Increasingly the desire grew in his heart to know that he himself had been pardoned from his sins and to know the joy of forgiveness. He realized that he was a sinner. He came to realize afresh that God hates sin. He read in the Gospel where Jesus said, "Repent ye, and believe the gospel" (Mark 1:15). The Heavenly Father did not mock this spiritually starved, lonely American boy. The light finally broke, and DeShazer knew - that salvation was his.

9.   The Miracle of Conversion

For days DeShazer, more or less unwittingly, had been moving toward the crisis point. The prayers of his parents certainly had followed him. The prayers of former friends had ascended to the throne of God in his behalf. The word of God through the precious Book had been illuminated by the Holy Spirit, and certainly the presence of Christ speaking to his inner consciousness and knocking at his heart's door had made an impression. But all of these factors would have been of no avail without DeShazer's meeting the conditions. This he did. The miracle of conversion took place June 8, 1944.

DeShazer had been reading Romans 10:9, "If thou shalt confess with thy mouth the Lord Jesus, and shalt believe in thine heart that God hath raised him from the dead, thou shalt be saved." He had read that passage many times, but on this particular day, somehow it became a power in his life. He laid hold upon it as the very word of God. In prayer he said: "Lord, though I am far from home and though I am in prison, I must have forgiveness."

As he meditated and prayed along this line, there came into his soul a divine joy, a soul rest, an inner witness that God for Christ's sake had forgiven him.

There was not much he could do with respect to changing his way of living. There came over him a sense that God wanted obedience. He was just simple enough to tell the Lord that he would obey. He yielded his spirit, his plans, his hopes, his aspirations. It was then he learned the truth which he has mentioned over and over since that time. "Obedience to God is the way to eternal life." In writing about his glorious experience on that happy day he says:

> My heart was filled with joy. I wouldn't have traded places with anyone at that time. Oh, what a great joy it was to know that I was saved, that God had forgiven me of my sins, and that I had become partaker of the divine nature" (II Peter 1:4). Though I was unworthy and sinful, I had "redemption through his blood, the forgiveness of sins, according to the riches of his grace" (Ephesians 1:7).
>
> Hunger, starvation, and a freezing cold prison cell no longer had horrors for me. They would be only for a passing moment. Even death could hold no threat when I knew that God

had saved me. Death is just one more trial that I must go through before I can enjoy the pleasures of eternal life. There will be no pain, no suffering, no sorrow, no loneliness in heaven. Everything will be perfect with joy forever. I had the promise of being like Jesus who is God's Son. In that day I will know all things, for I will then be a partaker of immortality.

The time when DeShazer would have to give up the copy of the Bible was drawing near. He memorized as much of the Scriptures as possible. He went over and over certain portions and memorized so as to keep them fresh in his mind. One is amazed at his ability under the circumstances to memorize so much and to have it for ready reference during the remaining fourteen months he was in prison.

Becoming a Christian, however, did not change the outward environment of DeShazer's life. He was still in prison. Perhaps he would never get out. He had the same guards, the same obligation to remain in solitary confinement, the same intolerable food, and the absence of fellowship.

But DeShazer had made his decision. He had believed on the Lord Jesus Christ. He had become a Christian. Now as a Christian he was going to do his best to live the way a Christian should.

He knew he had been weak in self-control and in willpower. In his early life he had been taught to love people and to be friendly to all. Seldom had he permitted himself to do this. In his reading of the Bible, he found much emphasis upon loving one another. He knew in other days he had been disobedient to his parents and that throughout the years he had been disobedient to God and to his own conscience. All of this was sin. But now through the grace of the Lord Jesus Christ he was forgiven for all those wrongs.

What he wanted now was divine strength. He wanted to strengthen his self-control and gain a new grip on his willpower. Many lessons were necessary for him to learn to trust the Lord. In John 1:12 he read, "As many as received him, to them gave he power to become the sons of God." It was that power which he needed and which he wanted.

He remembered the attitudes and feelings he had before his conversion. He remembered that just before his change of heart he had become very angry. One day during the period he was supposed to be cleaning his cell, one of the guards came along and yelled at him, "Hurry up." This made DeShazer angry, and almost before he knew it, he told the guard in English, "Go, jump in the lake." Naturally the guard didn't like this. DeShazer describes the incident:

Before I knew what was going to happen, the door was unlocked, and the guard hit me on the head with his fist. I immediately kicked him in the stomach with my bare foot, and he hit me with his steel scabbard. I had been using some water on the floor to mop up my cell. I picked up the dirty mop water and threw it on the guard. It cooled him off enough so that he didn't do any more than swear at me. But it is strange that he didn't cut off my head. This was not the way that I had been taught to make friends.

But that was before DeShazer accepted the way of Christ. After he became a Christian, his attitude changed. He knew it, and in due time his guards knew it, and so did his comrades. In John 13:34 Jesus said, "Love one another." Again DeShazer was seized with the meaning of obedience. He says:

> God expects us to keep His commandments. The only way we know we are saved is to keep the commandments of Christ. I found out when I read the Bible that it was necessary to be obedient. God hates sin and disobedience. We cannot please God if we continue doing those things that we know are wrong. If we accept Jesus and continue to sin, we will be like the seed in the parable which fell on stony ground and when it sprung up, because it had no depth of soil, soon withered and died (Matthew 13:3-9).
>
> When Jesus was on earth, He warned people not to be led astray by the human desire to do their own will. In Matthew 7:21 Jesus said, "Not every one that saith unto me, Lord, Lord, shall enter into the kingdom of heaven; but he that doeth the will of my Father which is in heaven." Obedience is what God has required from the beginning of the history of mankind. If we accept Jesus, we must be obedient or be cast out of the kingdom of God.
>
> When I memorized I John 2:3-6, I found it was necessary to be obedient. I wanted to know that I was a real Christian and not a hypocrite. These verses tell us we can know: "And hereby we do know that we know him, if we keep his commandments. He that saith, I know him, and keepeth not his commandments, is a liar, and the truth is not in him. But whoso keepeth his word, in him verily is the love of God perfected: hereby know we that we are in him. He that saith he abideth in him ought himself also to walk, even as he walked."
>
> Submission to Jesus brings a wonderful peace. I came to realize that my life would be more enjoyable if I were obedient. I found at first it was hard to do what I knew was right. I had much trouble for more than three weeks. The habits of swearing, thinking vulgar thoughts, and telling lies did not immediately leave me when I accepted Jesus. However, when the manifestations of

sin appeared I asked for forgiveness right away. The promise of I John 1:9 says, "If we confess our sins, he is faithful and just to forgive us our sins, and to cleanse us from all unrighteousness." God always keeps His promises, and since I did my part all unrighteousness was taken away.

Since DeShazer felt the command of God was to love his fellowmen, and since the only individuals he was privileged to meet were guards, he was waiting for an opportunity to demonstrate his love to them. An opportunity thus to test his newfound love and his determination to love others soon came. One day as he was being taken back to his cell by one of the guards, something happened which brought this matter very forcibly to his mind. For some reason the guard was in a special hurry. While they were on their way toward the cell, the guard slapped DeShazer on the back with his hand and ordered, *"Hiaku, hiaku!"* (Hurry up! hurry up!) When they came to the door of the cell, he opened the door a little and shoved DeShazer inside. Unfortunately, before DeShazer could get through the door, the guard slammed it and caught DeShazer's foot. Instead of opening the door to release his foot, the guard began kicking DeShazer's bare foot with his hobnailed boots. Finally, DeShazer was able to push the door open and get his foot free. He jumped inside. In recalling this incident, DeShazer admits that he felt resentment and hatred for the guard. Matthew 5:44 came to mind in which Jesus said, "Love your enemies, bless them that curse you, do good to them that hate you, and pray for them which despitefully use you, and persecute you."

Such an experience would be a real test to most new converts. In referring to this occasion DeShazer says:

> Jesus' words were coming to my mind, but at first I wished that I couldn't remember them. There was no way, however, by which I could get out of this predicament. I had promised obedience if God showed me the way. God had helped me to memorize the Sermon on the Mount so that He could use it to show me the way at this particular time. God was being faithful to show me the way. The only thing I could do was to submit and be obedient. Any other course would have meant God's displeasure, but by obedience God is pleased.

Other Scripture also came flooding DeShazer's mind: "Submit yourselves therefore to God. Resist the devil, and he will flee from you. Draw nigh to God, and he will draw nigh to you. Cleanse your hands, ye sinners; and purify your hearts, ye double minded. Be afflicted, and mourn, and weep: let your laughter be turned to mourning, and your joy to heaviness. Humble yourselves in the sight of the Lord, and he shall lift you up" (James 4:7-10).

Then, too, the thirteenth chapter of I Corinthians - the great love chapter - came to mind. Since being freed from prison, this is one of DeShazer's favorite passages. As a matter of fact, he quotes it perhaps more than any other portion of the Bible using, as a rule, James Moffat's translation: "Love is very patient, very kind. Love knows no jealousy; love makes no parade, gives itself no airs, is never rude, never selfish, never irritated, never resentful; love is never glad when others go wrong, love is gladdened by goodness, always slow to expose, always eager to believe the best, always hopeful, always patient. Love never disappears."

Herein lies the depth of DeShazer's consecration to return to Japan. The gospel truly meant to him, "Love your enemies." The way DeShazer put this in his own words is most interesting:

> I had seen people who could show a beautiful attitude in very trying circumstances, but I did not know that we can all have this kind of love that is long-suffering, kind, and patient. However, if we are given the commandment to love one another, it is surely possible for us actually to do so. Since God has given the commandment to love, our part of the transaction is to put forth an effort and try to have love for others. This would be a wonderful world if we would all try to love one another. If we would honestly try and if we would recognize Jesus as God's Son and our Savior, God will be pleased with us. I made up my mind to try.

So it was the very next morning after he had felt resentment and hatred for the guard who had kicked his foot, he had a chance to try to love someone, and in this instance, to love an enemy. As the guard came on duty, DeShazer moved toward the door of his cell and said, *"Ohayoo Gozaimasu"* (Good morning). Imagine the surprise of the guard. He looked in the direction of DeShazer with a puzzled expression. Perhaps he thought the prisoner had gone stark crazy. The guard, however, made no significant comment. Several mornings went by with DeShazer trying to be friendly.

One morning as the guard came on duty, he walked immediately over to DeShazer's cell and spoke to him through the door. He was smiling. DeShazer, at that time, knew but little Japanese, but he was able to talk to the guard enough to ask him how many brothers and sisters he had. This seemed to please the guard.

On another morning soon after this, he saw the guard walking up and down the corridor of the prison with his hands in a prayerful attitude and his lips moving. After a while the guard came over to DeShazer's cell and started to speak to him. He told him that he had been praying to his mother who had died when he was a small boy. This was in harmony with the guard's belief.

This particular guard became very friendly to DeShazer and from that time on did not shout at him nor treat him rudely. On one occasion, the guard slid back the little door and handed DeShazer a boiled sweet potato. This was a wonderful treat. DeShazer says he was already getting some payoff for being gracious to his enemies. At another time the guard gave him five figs and some candy. Again DeShazer was convinced that God's way is the best way. Moralizing on this he says:

> How easy it was to make a friend out of an enemy because I had just tried. God's way *will work* if we will try it out. Jesus was not an idealist whose ideals could not be realized. When He told us to love one another, He told us the best way to act, and it will work. His way will work out better than any other way which could be tried, but people and nations still try some other way to their own confusion.

10. Hot Summer/Cold Winter in Prison

Twenty-six months of grueling experience in a Japanese war prison weakened the health of DeShazer and his three comrades. The fact that DeShazer had accepted Christ gave him inner spiritual fortitude, but had not rebuilt his physical life. The summer of 1944 was extremely hot at Nanking. In the intense heat, the prison cells in the low wood frame buildings were almost unbearable in the daytime. Even at night it was so sultry it was difficult to rest. Conditions were further worsened by the inhumane manner of the prison construction. The doors were made of solid wood. There was no way to ventilate the cells, no circulation of air.

Lieutenant Hite became very ill with an extremely high fever. When it became apparent that his life was in jeopardy, the guards began to give him some attention. Apparently, they had been reprimanded for their carelessness in connection with the death of Lieutenant Meder. They replaced the solid wood door of his cell with a screen door. This made it possible for a passage of air through the little high window down through the door. In spite of this, Hite's fever continued dangerously high.

Much to the relief of Hite's comrades and, of course, to himself the Japanese officials began to take serious interest in his welfare and made an unusual effort to bring him back to health. A medical assistant was given the duty of looking after him. Apparently he was told to spare no effort to save him. DeShazer reports that often he could hear the Japanese bringing ice to put on Hite's feverish head. The young physician actually moved into the prison himself so that he could be near Hite in order to take care of him. Under the patient care of this young medical assistant and with the advent of cooler weather, Hite began to mend.

Throughout the unbearable days and nights of the summer of 1944, DeShazer received unusual encouragement and strength because of his newfound love. Within himself he had the witness of the presence of the Lord. Months had passed since he had read the Bible. But the Scripture that he memorized was becoming well known to him. The first Epistle of John was one of his favorites. He had memorized all five chapters and made special use of the teachings concerning abiding in the Lord. Again and again there recurred to his mind the importance of the commandments of God and the necessity of being *obedient*. Such scriptures were recalled as: "Hereby do we know that we know him, if we keep his commandments." DeShazer says concerning this truth, "I knew that I knew Him because I was able by the power He gives actually to keep His commandments."

Almost in a soliloquy he would become subjective and talk to himself along this line:

> That's a good method to tell whether anyone is a Christian. Anyone who keeps God's commandments is a Christian. I have faith that the blood of Jesus covers all of my sins. I know that Jesus died for me; consequently I can ask myself the question, "Am I doing what I think is right to the best of my ability or am I doing anything that I know is wrong, willfully?" If I am not willfully disobedient and I am trying to do what I know to be right, I am living up to all the light that God has given me. I am keeping His commandments, and the Bible says that I know Him if I keep His commandments.

During the long, hot summer, the hours of the days dragged slowly. The prisoners could look out the little window and see the blue sky. How they longed to get outside and fix their eyes on something besides the four walls of their cells. The few precious moments they were allowed outside each day were a great relief, but, oh, how quickly they passed!

Fall came with more moderate temperatures. Weeks passed, and finally the beginning of a very bad winter, the winter of 1944-45. There was a heavy snowfall the first of December. From that time on, there was snow in the prison yard until the first of March. It was the coldest winter the men experienced throughout their entire imprisonment.

The guards brought heavier clothes, and, as the winter became more severe, they finally returned to the men their old army clothes. These were put on over the Japanese garments. To the credit of the Japanese prison at Nanking it must be said that the men were able to keep their clothes much cleaner than in the prison at Shanghai. This was a new prison, and fortunately there were no lice. In the former prison, they were constantly plagued by the presence of lice. The only redeeming feature in connection with the lice was that it did occupy their time to quite an extent in hunting them out from their clothes and crushing them between their thumbnails.

It was two or three weeks after the first heavy snowfall before the guards took the men out into the prison yard for exercise. At this time the prisoners cleaned their cells. After they had finished, they were told to carry out some exercise but were warned not to take off their slippers. The slippers which they had, however, were the loose Japanese kind, and it was impossible for them to run without losing them. With snow on the ground it was impossible to exercise without jumping and running. They walked around the yard two or three times but were eager to run in order to get warmed up. (This was the only time of the day that they were able to get warm.) They finally ignored the order, kicked off their slippers, and started running barefooted.

There was a penalty to pay! As soon as the guards saw them running without their slippers, they ordered them to stop and go back into their cells. Naturally their feet were dirty since in some of the places where they had been running the snow had melted and the ground was muddy. The men started for the building expecting to go inside to wash their feet at the water hydrant. The guards, however, rushed them away and told them to go over to the snowbank and clean their feet in the snow.

The men told the guards that they would rather wash their feet at the water hydrant. Still the guards insisted that they go to the snowbank. Lieutenant Barr, resenting their orders, tried to go inside. One of the guards grabbed him and tried to turn him around by taking hold of his coat sleeve. Barr, however, with considerable energy jabbed his elbow into the guard's stomach. This made the guards even more angry, and Lieutenant Barr was kept outside after his comrades were taken to their cells.

Lieutenant Barr paid dearly for his deed. About ten guards began beating him. To their surprise Lieutenant Barr, six feet two inches tall, was more alert and stronger than they expected. Not disposed to submit willingly to a whipping, Barr gave the guards a rather rough time. Finally, they were able to shove him along and put him into his cell. Then it was that the captain of the prison was called to help give discipline. Barr was placed in a straitjacket, his arms tied behind his back, and ropes were drawn so tight that his shoulder nearly broke. His chest, too, was subjected to such awful tension by the ropes around his body that the pain was excruciating. To the other men it sounded as if Barr was being killed. He was certainly doing a good job of hollering.

The screaming was undoubtedly due to the physical torture, but it also had a wholesome, psychological effect on the prison official, who, according to DeShazer, "was really a kindhearted, tender-spirited man." One of the guards, Mr. Misaka, who had tried to be a gentleman and a good friend made an effort to persuade the others to release Barr. This they did after about one hour of torture. The guards seemed to feel rather virtuous, for they told Lieutenant Barr that he was fortunate because they tortured their own men by that means for four to six hours when they had occasion to discipline them.

The Barr incident once again brought dejection of spirit among the prisoners. They wondered whether there ever would be an end to prison life and the recurrence of such experiences. Fortunately, it was only a short time before their hopes were again lifted. This time it was more than better food or a kindly guard. The most welcome news of many, many months came on Christmas Day, 1944. It seems impossible that the appearance of bombers could be a welcome sound and sight, but such it was for these American flyers when for the first time they realized that American dive bombers had reached Nanking. The elation of the prisoners was almost unbounded. They actually saw the dive bombers skimming over the housetops, shooting as they came. They heard the Japanese shooting back at them, apparently with every weapon that they could procure. Soon they heard bombs exploding and saw clouds of black smoke billowing toward the sky. Evidently some oil refineries and storage tanks had been the targets.

The satisfaction which came to the minds of the prisoners when they knew that Americans were deep in China was inexpressible. For many months the Japanese guards had been telling them extreme stories regarding the losses of the United States and the successes of the Japanese. Repeatedly they would say that the Japanese had taken possession of San Francisco and New York, that Japanese soldiers were marching up and down the streets of these and other cities giving orders to the American people. Secretly, of course, the American airmen looked for the appearance of American airplanes. Month after month came and went without any such appearance. Sometimes they wondered whether the stories told by the guards were true.

Evidently the Japanese officials believed their own stories, for they were taken completely by surprise by the appearance of the American planes. They were able, quickly, to adjust to the situation, for they were soon telling the Americans that the United States planes had dropped a few bombs in the rivers and killed a few fish. The thought of Japan ever having to surrender seemed completely foreign to their thinking. The American planes, however, brought no relief to the intense cold inside the Japanese prison. The long, cold winter continued. DeShazer and his comrades constantly suffered with colds. DeShazer began breaking out with large boils. Sometimes boils appeared on the bottoms of his feet. These continued through the remainder of the winter. When warmer weather came, the boils disappeared for a time but reappeared later in the summer.

For some reason not known to the American airmen they were made ready for another long overland trip. It was the middle of June when one morning they were taken out of their cells, once again handcuffed and tied up in preparation for the move. It must have been interesting to see the guards shake hands with the men in this handcuffed position. Despite the fact that one group was guards and the other was prisoners there had been built up a real sense of friendship. They had been together in the Nanking prison from April 1943, to the middle of June 1945 -- more than twenty-six months. This was a full year after DeShazer's conversion.

They rode by train in a northerly direction for more than forty hours. They did not know where they were going. They were traveling through strange country and seeing strange crowds. Their hands and legs were tied with their belts. Each man had a guard who hung on to the rope whether they were sitting or standing. Over each man was a large green raincoat. Over each head was pulled a hat which had a mask for a face.

The train was crowded beyond all description. Most of the passengers were soldiers. Some, however, were civilians, and some were Red Cross workers. All of the women were out in the aisles sitting on the floor or on some of the baggage. The men in the Japanese program are the ones who occupy the seats. High-ranking officers came into the car and ordered those of lower rank to get up and give them a place. Sometimes Chinese men or women tried to get through the car, but someone ordered them out, and, if they didn't understand, a slap of the hand convinced them that they were to stay out. The whole group, however, seemed to be a serious, tired-looking crowd of people.

Everyone was surprised to see the prisoners wearing the peculiar masks, but no one dared to ask questions. DeShazer describes an incident which seemed to him amusing:

> A Japanese mother brought her two children up rather close to our masked faces. While the children with surprised faces were looking at us, the mother for sheer fun silently moved away. As the children looked at us and our peculiar masks, they screamed out in fright. This caused everyone in the train to laugh, and the mother returned smiling to comfort her children.

In this grotesque situation, DeShazer was not unmindful of his dedication to God. He says:

> While riding on the train, I remembered the Bible message. I wondered what God was going to do with all of these souls as these people didn't know Jesus. They had probably never heard of Him. I thanked God for His mercy to me in allowing me the privilege of reading the Bible. I was glad for a Christian home and my parents' prayers which God had heard. I wished there was some way the people on the train could know about the salvation which God had provided for all people. What joy they would know if Jesus were dwelling in their hearts as He was dwelling in mine!

After nearly three days of thus journeying in a strange country, shackled down, and with hoods over their faces, they arrived in Peking. Just before coming into the station, the guards told the prisoners where they were. It was an extremely hot day, and, after leaving the train, the prisoners were taken to the side of the station to wait in a shady place for a military truck. People seemed to be everywhere. Many Chinese were lying in the shade of the railroad station. As the guards with their prisoners came near, these loafers were told to clear out and make way.

One old Chinese lady who had a great deal of baggage was unable to get out of the way rapidly enough. One of the Japanese officers started screaming at the woman to hurry. Obviously, the poor woman was hurrying as fast as her age would allow. This, however, was not sufficient. The officer went over and slapped her on both sides of the face in an effort to make her really hurry. This treatment seemed to be common almost everywhere. DeShazer says, "It made me wish that they could be shown the way of love."

Finally, a truck came and took the guards and prisoners to a large prison in Peking. Apparently it was a military prison with more than one thousand Japanese prisoners receiving typical oriental punishment for some misconduct. Five or six of the Japanese soldier prisoners were placed in a prison cell together and for two hours were forced to kneel on the floor without changing position. After such a two hour period they were all supposed to sit on the floor, straight up, feet out in front, without any support for their backs.

The situation around Peking was decidedly different from that the Americans had experienced around Nanking. The guards at Nanking were constantly talking about the people having a higher standard of living than the Chinese. They were frequently claiming that Japan was the leading nation in the world for cleanliness and decency. After having traveled some six hundred miles deeper into China, DeShazer admits that he could see why the Japanese felt their manner of living was better than that of the Chinese. At the same time the American airmen were trying to tell the guards how much better things were in America. DeShazer says:

> We tried to tell them about the food and the automobiles, but it seemed like a fairy tale to them. They thought America was a place where bandits flourished and waxed rich. Soldiers in the Japanese Army were accustomed to being slapped by an officer of higher rank. When we told them there was no slapping in the U. S. Army, they said that was impossible, for they thought there would be no discipline.

The American prisoners were no longer to have the joy of even a prison courtyard. The poor, persecuted Chinese might be everywhere through the city of Peking, but the quartet of Americans were placed in the inner section of this Japanese military prison. Each one was placed in a solitary cell, and from that time on there was no more going outside for exercise. The only time they were to see each other at all was when they were allowed to get together for a bath, once a week.

Very frequently the Americans could hear and occasionally see the guards take the soldiers out of their cells and beat them. This apparently was one of their chief methods of keeping discipline. It was difficult for DeShazer to think he was in a real world. There was so much cruelty and fear. He was constantly reminded that freedom is one of the great heritages in the United States not known in a non-Christian country.

11.   Near Death

When the American prisoners were first put into solitary confinement in the Peking Japanese prison, they were forced to sit on the floor just as the other prisoners were. The American men, however, were not accustomed to sitting on the floor. The whole experience became so excruciating that the guards were finally persuaded to provide some relief. Relief it was to the men under the circumstances, but, when we think of this arrangement in ordinary life, it seems unbearable.

Sometimes DeShazer refers to the relief that was provided in terms of a "bench". A small bench, he says, was provided for each of the American men to sit on. The facts are, it was far from a bench, for it was essentially a little stool with a top made of a two by four, about eight inches long. Throughout the entire day each man was required to sit three feet from the wall and keep his face toward the rear wall. Evidently, the Japanese did not want the Americans to see some of the brutal treatment which their own soldiers received.

Many people even in normal health, subjected to this kind of treatment, would undoubtedly crack up mentally in a short time. It is difficult to imagine the mental torment experienced by these men who had gone through thirty-eight months of deprivation, hunger, sickness, and punishment. With DeShazer, one month was all he could stand. Already his body was weakened by severe attacks of dysentery; he was much emaciated. Boils appeared again - this time all over his body. He reports that he counted as many as seventy-five bad boils at one time. Of course, he was no longer able to sit on the little stool. He lay on his bed mat day after day.

After about three weeks of this he became somewhat delirious. He was a very sick man; he describes his condition as follows:

> I still kept going over the verses in the Bible that I had memorized. I thought it wouldn't be long before I would be in heaven with Lieutenant Meder. My heart was hurting, and I could remember how Lieutenant Meder said his heart had hurt before he died. Several of the Nanking prison guards had told me the reason Meder died was that his heart had stopped. I thought I would probably die for the same reason.

Experiences of this kind went on for several days. Finally Matthew

17:20 came to mind. "If ye have faith as a grain of mustard seed, ye shall say unto this mountain, Remove hence to yonder place; and it shall remove; and nothing shall be impossible unto you." He began to think about how small a mustard seed is, and then he thought, "Surely I have that much faith - that God can make me well!"

Apparently, the Holy Spirit was leading him into a new experience. His comment regarding what he went through is most gripping. Many, undoubtedly, would not understand it. Without doubt, the blessed Holy Spirit understanding his weakened condition came and, like the ministering angels with Christ himself in Gethsemane, ministered unto him:

> Many times I had thanked God for faith to believe that I was saved. When I had just believed, then God had shown me that I was saved. It now seemed to me that God wished for me to have the faith that He would heal me from my bad attack of dysentery. God had been such a good friend to me that I felt I could not act as a coward now. The only thing to do was to try it out and see if God was really talking to me.
>
> I got out of bed and sat on the little bench one morning after I had prayed it all out with God. I was so weak that my heart could have stopped very easily, but God knows how to keep a person's heart going. I didn't know what to expect. I just prayed that God would make me better. I made up my mind to sit there until I either passed out or God healed me.
>
> It was not long before the voice of God broke into my thoughts. This was different from anything I had experienced before. I had often wondered where a person's thoughts come from, and as I sat in prison I used to be conscious of the activity of my thoughts. Ordinarily, I had control over them, but now it was different. I still had control over my thoughts, yet I knew that I was being possessed by another power. I was sure I was not responsible for the thoughts coming to my mind. I had never dreamed of anything like this. It was hard for me to realize that I was experiencing such a glorious contact with God.
>
> "It is the Holy Spirit who is speaking to you," the mysterious voice said. "The Holy Spirit has made you free." I immediately began to wonder if I was going to get out of prison. The voice said, "You are free to do as you please. You can go through the wall or jump over the wall. You are free." I couldn't figure that out, but I had only a desire to do what was pleasing to God. "The Holy Spirit has set you free from sin," I was told.
>
> Free from sin! Yes, God's Word has said, "Whosoever abideth in him sinneth not: whosoever sinneth hath not seen him, neither known him." This was in the first Epistle of John that I had

memorized. It was the third chapter and sixth verse. I was free from any desire to do willful sin. If I knew something was wrong, I would put forth every effort I could not to do it any more. James 4:17 states, "Therefore to him that knoweth to do good, and doeth it not, to him it is sin." This is the kind of sin that God expects us to live above today. The sin of ignorance spoken of in Leviticus is all taken care of by the blood of Jesus. We have been given power by Jesus to be free from willful, disobedient sin.

I was able to tell by this reasoning that the voice speaking to me agreed with the Bible. The Spirit and the Word agree. I was almost too happy for this world. I had been lonesome and sick, but now God spoke to me and filled my heart with an unearthly joy.

I found out that I could ask questions and I could receive answers right away. This was a big help to me in connection with my food. I was always hungry, but, often, if I ate the food, I would become very sick. When the food came to the door, I would pray and ask if I should eat the food or should send it back. If the voice said, "Yes, yes," I would eat; but if the answer was, "No, no," I would send the food back. For two days I was not given permission to eat or to drink. I was weak, but the sickness was leaving me.

I would not lie down in the daytime if I was not sure that it was permissible for me to do so. My body was tired and weak, but I wanted to be sure and show "faith as a grain of mustard seed." As I was sitting on the little seat facing the wall, I wondered if there wasn't some way that I could let the guards know about the wonderful spirit of Jesus which was so present with me. His power and life were throbbing with a thrilling consciousness to me at every heartbeat.

There didn't seem to be much that I could do, but I remembered the story about Daniel. I went down on my knees in front of the door, folded my hands to pray, and I really did pray. The first guard came by, beat on the door with his sword and hollered at me to get back on my bench. It was against the rules for any prisoner even to look at the door. Japanese prisoners received a beating for such audacity, but I did not move when the guard shouted. I felt no fear since God had shown me what to do. I felt a great weight of joy.

In a very short time the guard returned with several other guards. The door opened and the guards walked into my cell. They never hit me nor hollered at me. They acted a little awed. A medical man came to my cell, and I was picked up and laid down on a straw mat. The medical man rolled up my shirt sleeve and shot some medicine into my arm, after which I was left alone in my cell to thank Jesus who was close by my side.

When mealtime came, I was surprised to receive a nice pint of milk, boiled eggs, some good well-made bread, and some nice, nourishing soup. I couldn't help crying and laughing when I thought how beautifully and wonderfully God had worked all this out for me. From that time until we were released from prison, I received milk, eggs, bread, and good nourishing food. I stayed in bed because I thought that God had indicated that this was thing for me to do.

The foregoing experience was wonderful in every way to DeShazer. Next to his wonderful experience of conversion some fourteen months before, this was the most wonderful spiritual experience he had ever enjoyed.

On August 10, 1945, he had another type of experience which will always remain sacred to him. He says that on this notable day when he first woke up in the morning he was told to "start praying."

I asked, "What shall I pray about?" Pray for peace, and pray without ceasing, I was told. I had prayed about peace but very little, if at all, before that time, as it seemed useless. I thought God could stop the war any time with the power which He had manifested.

But God was now teaching me the lesson of cooperation. It was God's joy for me to be willing to let Him use me. God does use human instruments to accomplish His will here on earth. It will be a great joy to us through all eternity if we can cooperate with Him. I started to pray for peace, although I had a very poor idea of what was taking place in the world at that time.

About seven o'clock in the morning I began to pray. It seemed very easy to pray on the subject of peace. I prayed that God would put a great desire in the hearts of the Japanese leaders for peace. I thought about the days of peace that would follow. Japanese people would no doubt be discouraged, and I felt sympathetic toward them. I prayed that God would not allow them to fall into persecution by the victorious armies.

At two o'clock in the afternoon the Holy Spirit told me, "You don't need to pray anymore. The victory is won." I was amazed. I thought this was quicker and better than the regular method of receiving world news. Probably this news broadcast had not come over the radio to America as yet. I thought I would just wait and see what was to happen.

DeShazer, of course, had no radio. He was not privileged for several days to get the news of that fateful tenth day of August 1945. We now know that that was the day the first atomic bomb was dropped on Hiroshima. It was then that the Japanese leaders began to sue for peace. He learned about this later, and once again he was convinced that God had been teaching him a lesson in cooperation. From that day forward he began to put stress upon the fact that God wants us to pray, that God hears and answers prayer, that God knows the best way.

The next ten days and nights constitute a most interesting period in DeShazer's life of continuous joy. He says:

> I felt the love of God flooding my soul. Night and day a rapturous joy was being experienced. I felt certain that I was having a foretaste of heaven.

At the same time new strength was coming to his weakened body. He was now receiving plenty of good food. Vitality was returning. It was almost sheer ecstasy as he lay on his straw mat to realize both the wonder of returning physical strength and at the same time to experience the joy of the fullness of the Holy Spirit.

> I promised God that I would make restitution for the things that I had stolen. I felt certain that I would be able to return to the United States. I was going to make amends as far as God showed me it was the right thing to do. It was a wonderful feeling not to harbor any resentment or ill will toward anyone. I felt love toward the Japanese people and a deep interest in their welfare. I felt that we were all made by the same God and that we must share our hardships and our happiness together. How I wished that I could tell the Japanese people about Jesus! I knew that my Saviour would be their Saviour, too. I realized that Jesus died for our sins, that He was alive today, and that He died so that He might become our Savior. He is coming back again to reign as our King for ever and ever. Jesus was as real and alive to me as anyone could possibly be.

He had news from heaven that the victory was won. As yet, however, no word had been received from any guard concerning developments. One day, looking out the window, he saw smoke and burnt paper rising up in the sky. As the guards came on duty, he noticed they were wearing new clothes. He saw them discarding old clothes and breaking into their supplies. He felt that these were the first signs that the end had come.

His heart beat faster and faster as he thought about the freedom that would soon be his. Then his thoughts were directed to the Japanese.

I could not help wondering what would happen to Japan now. Their hopes had been set on victory. It would be an awful blow to suffer defeat. But, if the Japanese found out about Jesus, the military defeat to them would in reality be a great victory. At this time the voice of the Holy Spirit spoke to me clearly: "You are called to go and teach the Japanese people and to go wherever I send you."

It seemed difficult for him to believe that God would call him to such an important work. He knew he had never had any ability as a public speaker. He knew he had lacked training and Bible study. He recalled that he had always seemed to be, "as dry as a rock," when he wanted to tell something. At the same time he realized that he had promised God that he would do God's will. Once more in his inner soul he agreed that he would cooperate with the Lord.

I thought perhaps I could be a janitor in some church, but God's voice was telling me, "Get in and work for all you are worth. You have as good a chance as anyone else." I knew that I could try, and I had already been shown the power of Jesus, if we have "faith as a grain of mustard seed."

12.   Freedom at Last

On August 20, 1945, just ten days after his wonderful experience of praying for peace, freedom came to DeShazer and his comrades. Forty months of imprisonment and punishment abruptly came to an end! A Japanese official announced, "The war is over. You can go home now." Those were wonderful words. The cells were opened. The men came out. This was the first time the Americans had seen each other for several weeks.

Immediately they noticed that there were but three. Lieutenant George Barr was not with them. At first they were afraid that he had died. Later, however, Barr joined the group. He had been seriously ill. Two Japanese guards were helping him walk. The other three were very weak and thin, but the look of joy and happiness was seen in their hollow eyes as they greeted one another and listened to the head official again say, "The war is over. You can go home now."

The Japanese guards offered to give each a haircut. This was refused since they knew it would be a close clip to the scalp. Expecting to be back soon in America, they did not want to appear with a prisoner's haircut. They were given their old army clothes -- now more than three years old -- which they had been wearing when they were captured. They were then loaded on a truck and taken to a big English hotel. Everywhere they looked they saw moving crowds. Excitement prevailed. The men were fairly in a daze. At the same time they were anxious to get all the news possible. DeShazer says:

> Everyone came to look at us, and some people tried to tell us the news. So many things were happening so fast I couldn't seem to keep up with everything. After someone talked, I couldn't remember what he had said. My mind wasn't working right.

In spite of the fact that for some weeks DeShazer had been receiving better food while in prison, he thought his first meal as a free man was a wonderful treat. Like all hungry people, these half-starved men looked forward to eating good, rich food. Now they had their opportunity! When reporting on it, they said, "We ate all of the Irish stew we could hold." The doctors gave them vitamin pills and shot vitamin fluid into their arms. The food they ate digested well and rapidly brought new strength.

In the open with other people, they were able quickly to get the gist of the war news. They heard about the atomic bomb. They learned that

American parachute troops had flown in to rescue them. They were told the war had ended on the fifteenth of August, but DeShazer says, I remember the time God had said the victory was won." The parachute rescue group came boldly into the Peking area. They had asked the Japanese officials where the Doolittle flyers were held. It seems the American Secret Service was able to find out about them and their location. But the Japanese official answered their query by saying that all had been executed.

Without doubt, it will never be known exactly how word did get out that some of the Doolittle flyers, as prisoners, were still alive. DeShazer has an interesting explanation concerning it. They think it was made possible through some U. S. Marines who were imprisoned near them in Nanking. Some of the soup brought to the prisoners was in aluminum teacups. One day Lieutenant Nielson noticed that on the bottom of one teacup was written, "U. S. Marines."

Nielson made up his mind that some of the cups brought to them had at times been taken to the marines. He thought perhaps some of the cups they were using would in turn be taken back to the marines. Nielson told his comrades about it, so they picked up some nails in the yard, sharpened them on the cement walls, and started corresponding with the marines by writing on the bottoms of the aluminum teacups. Their method of corresponding was not noticed for about two months. Their plan, however, was successful, for word had gone to the marines concerning the four Doolittle flyers in solitary confinement.

The U. S. Marines in prison had been captured at the very first of the war. After several months in a concentration camp, they decided to escape. Ten men tried to get away, but only three succeeded. The other seven were put into prison near the Doolittle men. The dishes these marines used had made the rounds in the furtive correspondence.

The marines were the first to be released when the war ended. They were thus able to tell the American parachute officers that some of the Doolittle flyers were still alive. In view of this, when the Japanese officers told the parachute officers that all the Doolittle men had been executed, they knew otherwise. By putting on the pressure, the parachute men were able to find the prisoner's location and to get their release.

Following their release, the Doolittle men were now in a big hotel with many other people. These were businessmen and ex-policemen who were held in concentration camps during the war. These concentration camps were entirely different from the prisons where the Doolittle men were confined. As a rule, the people in the concentration camps were free to move around in their confined area. Quite often they received Red Cross packages from allied countries. Some of the English policemen were greatly pleased by the kindness shown by the American Red Cross. They told the Doolittle men that the packages from the United States contained the best food and were packed in such a way that nothing of significant value could have been added to the package.

The released men were given candy and concentrated food out of some of the packages flown in by the U. S. Army. In looking back on it, DeShazer rather humorously says:

> We would take the food that we couldn't eat and store it away in case we became hungry before mealtime. It just seemed the natural thing to do. But after a while some of the people would laugh and ask us if we were getting ready for another famine. It seemed hard to realize that we were free and would not need to suffer from hunger pangs anymore.

A further instance which shows the extent to which the Doolittle flyers were thinking of food took place on the second day of their freedom. It seems that an American woman came to see the men at the Peking Hotel. She and her husband, a French man who had been engaged in business in China before the war, had been in China since the opening of hostilities. This American woman said that she would like to do something for the Doolittle flyers. DeShazer says:

> She asked us what we would like. The other fellows asked me to say, so I told the lady that I could not think of anything better than a dish of ice cream. She said that was what we would get, and she would make it herself. The next day we ate a freezer full of ice cream which was a real treat to us.

On the third day, American B-24s landed on the airfield of the defeated Japanese, and the next day three of the flyers were flown to Chungking. Lieutenant Barr had to stay at Peking since his health would not permit an airplane trip. He later returned to America by steamship.

The wonderful news of finding four of the Doolittle flyers was released to the world on August 20. The first word which came over the American radio that morning said that four had been found alive but did not give their names. For some hours the suspense in the heart of a little mother in Salem, Oregon, was indescribable. She had prayed and prayed. She had trusted the Lord through forty long months, but still there was an inner longing for an outward evidence that her prayers had been answered. Was it possible? Would it be true that one of the four would be her own Jake? Ears were glued to the radio anxiously waiting for further word. This further word came about noon when to the inexpressible joy of mother, stepfather, half sister, other relatives, and many, many friends, announcement was made that one of the four was Sergeant Jacob DeShazer.

At the same time there was deep sorrow and sympathy for others who, too, were waiting that forenoon for a good word, only once again to be brokenhearted when they learned that their loved one was not among the four. Such was the case in the homes of Lieutenant Hallmark, Lieutenant Farrow, and the machine-gunner Spaatz, who had been so mercilessly executed by the Japanese after six months of indescribable torture in prison; also in the homes of the bombardier and the rear gunner who drowned after the crash landing of Lieutenant Hallmark's plane off the China coast.

The great joy which came to DeShazer's mother upon learning that her son was alive and free was unbounded. It seemed that it would be impossible for anything more wonderful to take place. Imagine her added joy when word came over the airwaves that Jake not only had been converted while in prison but that he had decided to give the rest of his life to missionary work. The newspaper men seemed to think this was even greater news than his deliverance from prison. Pictures of DeShazer on his knees were radioed throughout the world. Some said the young man was only seeking the limelight. Others said it was undoubtedly a sincere statement but would be short-lived.

The released joyful flyers were flown home by way of India and across the Atlantic Ocean. As soon as DeShazer landed in Washington, D. C., he sent word to his parents. He told them of his conversion and also of his intention to return to Japan as a missionary.

It was early September when the party landed on American soil. They were taken immediately to Walter Reed Hospital. As might be expected, they were subjected to many interviews with newspaper men. The released flyers soon learned that much publicity had been given to the Doolittle raid and that the public wanted to know about their prison experiences. Various newspaper men offered large sums of money for their story. DeShazer with others went to New York and spoke on "We the People" radio program. At that time DeShazer received $400 for reading one sentence over the radio. He says, "It is the most I have ever been paid for opening my mouth."

He received $2,250 from a newspaper syndicate for his personal story. He also received back pay for the forty months he had been in prison which amounted to $5,600. He says:

> I felt that I was a very wealthy person when I told Lieutenant Hite and Lieutenant Nielson good-bye and boarded an airplane in Washington, D. C., to go to the home of my parents in Salem, Oregon.

Before leaving for the West, however, a notable thing took place at a fashionable night spot in New York City. Years later this was featured in a nationwide radio broadcast by the news commentator, Lowell Thomas. He spoke on the occasion of the eighth anniversary reunion of Doolittle's "Tokyo Raiders" at Palm Desert, California, in the spring of 1950. Mr.

Thomas' tribute to DeShazer gave testimony to the world regarding DeShazer and his stand for personal righteousness:

> Sergeant DeShazer, one of the eighty original Tokyo raiders, was one of the fliers unfortunate enough to be captured by the Japanese. Three of the prisoners were executed and one starved to death. The other four went through a bitter ordeal. They came home after the war, and one thing that happened was a gay glittering party at New York's fashionable Stork Club. Colonel Ross Greening, pilot of the eleventh bomber in that famous takeoff, was sitting beside DeShazer. They were having champagne, and Greening noticed that Jake was merely toying with his glass.
>
> "You're not drinking," said the colonel. "How come?"
>
> Jake thought a minute and replied, "I knew you'd ask me that, Ross, and I'll tell you about it."
>
> "He told me," relates Greening, "how the Japs kept him in a dark cell -- thirty-six months of solitary confinement -- and there, day after day, week after week, he could only sit and brood. Then, one day, the black hole was filled suddenly with brilliant light. And Jake heard a voice telling him that it should be his mission to teach the Japanese how to treat human beings decently. The light and the voice were a command, bidding him to do his bit in bringing Christianity to the Japanese." Greening's own impression was deepened and confirmed by a fellow prisoner of DeShazer in that Japanese jail. The two had long discussions of DeShazer's experience and did much to convince the other Doolittle fliers of the depth and meaning of it.
>
> Jake DeShazer resolved to become a missionary to Japan. He studied at Seattle Pacific College and went to spread the gospel in the country which had treated him so badly. Greening told of huge crowds who have heard Jake preach in Japan. In all of his work, he has had the support of his Doolittle buddies, and now the raiders have voted to support DeShazer's mission to Japan. That was the "main objective" of the 1950 reunion of the men who electrified the Allied cause and blasted the Japanese capital eight years ago.

Such experiences brought DeShazer face to face with life decisions. He states that while flying across America to the west coast, the Lord spoke to him very definitely regarding his own life and conduct. Here it was that he promised God never again to touch alcohol or tobacco. He says, "I felt an urge to get busy with the work that God had called me to do."

Great was the joy to Jake and to the entire family when he finally reached home at Salem, Oregon. At the family altar he had heard prayer as a lad and during the years of his youth. Here also during his absence prayers had been ascending in his behalf.

The Bible was read and prayer offered every morning in that home since Jake had dropped out of sight. Through sympathy and interest many friends of the parents joined them in prayer. Now great was the rejoicing. Family prayer was continued in the home, but another member had been added. Jake remembered the earlier days when he had heard the Bible read and they had met for family worship. He remembered in his early youth how he rebelled against this daily activity, but how different it was now! Friends gathered at the home and were present for morning worship. One very close friend was Mrs. J. R. Stewart. Jake, on his knees, listened while his parents and this guest prayed. When they finished Jake tried to pray, but he says, "Though I tried real hard, I couldn't get the praise I felt in my heart to come out in the words."

After the prayer service when they stood up, Jake told the others he wished he could pray as they did. They encouraged him and explained that in due time he would have no difficulty in being able to pray.

In that home during the next few days there was much joy and a constant spirit of thanksgiving. Along with this was the desire to see Jake, who was nearly starved, brought back to normal physical condition. Like any mother, Mrs. Andrus spent much time preparing good food. Nothing was spared in providing wholesome, appetizing, and enjoyable meals. The first twenty days out of prison he gained an average of one pound a day.

When Jake left home in 1940 for army service, his people were living in Madras, Oregon. In his absence they had retired from the farm and moved to Salem, Oregon. Jake was anxious to go back to his old hometown at Madras. He made such a trip, and great was the celebration held in his honor. He was given a watch and asked to make a speech. He says:

> It was a good place to begin my speech making so I told as much as I could about the prison and about the salvation I had received when I read the Bible. I ran out of wind pretty fast. I was sweating and working harder than I had ever worked in my life. It seems funny now, but I was nearly thirty-three years old, and this was my first public speech. In bed alone that night I prayed to God. I felt comfort from Him and a promise of victory if I would continue to try.

On his return trip to Salem, he was given two more opportunities to speak. One of these was at a youth rally where Dr. Nathan Cohen Beskin, a converted Russian Jew, was the main speaker. He spoke again at an Evangelical Church. Without doubt these experiences were of great help to DeShazer since it assisted him in putting himself on record and strengthening his commitment to God. He admitted that it was getting easier to speak. Still speech making continued to be a real task and somewhat of a cross.

He was supposed to have been given a ninety-day leave from the Army. However, within two weeks after arriving home he received a telegram asking him to report to Santa Ana Air Base in California. After reporting there he immediately asked for a discharge from the Army. To his surprise he was informed that it would be impossible to get out for some time since there was a large number of soldiers to be discharged.

Not having anything to do and having essential freedom, he did considerable visiting around Santa Ana. This was of particular interest since he had several relatives in that area. He was called upon to speak at various church and youth services. At one church someone asked him whether he had ever been baptized. He responded that he had been baptized, but not publicly. He recalled that while he was in prison he had wished that he could be baptized. He also recalled that at that time in rather strange simplicity he had actually gone over to one side of his prison cell where the wind was blowing the water from the eaves through the window and had stood in this spattering rain and praised God for a water baptism. He remembers this experience with much joy. He is thankful to these Christians for their zeal and their help to his Christian faith.

While he was at Santa Ana, a military blunder was committed by a leading official. This received nationwide publicity. There happened to be some fifty soldiers in this particular camp who had been prisoners of war. One of the most outstanding was DeShazer himself. Here was a man just released from the nightmare of solitary confinement, devastating disease, and semi-starvation. For no reason he was told to report for K. P. duty. He was assigned to cleaning dishes. While he was in the act of carrying dishes, a newspaper man came in and without authorization took DeShazer's picture as he, weak and emaciated, was carrying a large tray of dishes. This picture appeared in one of the leading Los Angeles papers. Naturally, it aroused a great deal of public sentiment against the military authorities for putting DeShazer and other former prisoners of war at menial tasks. The officials responsible for the blunder were given a reprimand. As a result, DeShazer was sent immediately to a hospital for further observation and care. It also resulted in stepping up the effort in getting a discharge. Just before he was sent to the hospital, he was called in to see the commanding officer who admitted that it had been a great mistake for him to be put on K. P. duty. The commanding officer also told him that he would do everything possible to help. Again DeShazer was made to praise the Lord for this further evidence of the guiding hand of his Heavenly Father.

13. Missionary Training Course

DeShazer had finished his high school work in May 1931. To anyone having been out of school fourteen years, it would be a real test of courage and determination to return again to the classroom. Add to this the experiences of several years in the Army and more than three years in prison without books or reading, and it is difficult to imagine the handicap confronting DeShazer in attempting to carry out his plan to train for missionary service.

Things, however, were moving very rapidly in his life. The fact that he had announced through the news reports his intention to train and go back to Japan as a missionary brought literature and catalogs from dozens of colleges and school from all parts of America. His sister, Helen, was a student at Seattle Pacific College. This provided a natural open door in that direction. Then too, Helen was secretary to President Watson. She had gone to the new home of her parents in Salem, Oregon, to greet Jake. Under date of September 13, 1945, she wrote to President Watson:

> My brother reached home about midnight last night. You can well imagine that there is not a happier home in the world than ours. He looks better than we had feared - has gained some fifteen pounds since being rescued. The most wonderful part of all, of course, is his experience with God and desire to return to Japan as a missionary after proper training. We are anxious to hear from his own lips what the news stories have said about God's communing with him during his time in solitary confinement.
>
> Naturally, I am hoping that SPC will be his choice of a college, but we will be happy with whatever decision he makes.

On September 20, President Charles Hoyt Watson of Seattle Pacific College wrote DeShazer in part:

> DEAR JACOB: I trust you will allow me to address you by your first name; since Helen has been my secretary this summer, I have come to feel very close to you. We greatly appreciate what you and your comrades have done. I am sure God now has a plan whereby you can use the tragic experiences of the last forty months for the uplift and salvation of many. We pray God's blessing upon you as you go forward in fellowship with the Lord.

I have just received a card from Helen. She indicated you were anxious to get started immediately with your school program. Be assured of our willingness and desire to cooperate in every way.

In the midst of conflicting desires and varied advices, DeShazer was not exactly sure what to do. Part of the time he thought he would wait until after he was discharged from the army before starting to school. As he now looks back on developments, he says that the Lord led in a wonderful way. Calls were coming in from various sections of the West for him to come as a speaker. One of these calls was from north central Washington at Okanogan where the Revered Mr. Finkbeiner was pastor. This man had been a good friend of DeShazer years before at Madras, Oregon. DeShazer accepted this invitation and while making the trip stopped off at Seattle Pacific College to visit his sister, Helen, who had returned to her work in President Watson's office.

As would be expected Helen introduced her brother to the president of the college. DeShazer describes this brief interview:

President Watson asked me when I was going to start to school. I said I didn't think I could go to school before the winter quarter, but he gave me a good chance to start immediately if I so desired. The result was that the next day I started college.

Thus it was that approximately two months after DeShazer had been released from prison he was back in school again. Speaking of this he says:

Think of it! Only three months before the time I started to school I had been seriously ill and thought I was going to die. God had healed me from sickness, baptized me with the Holy Spirit, and provided everything I needed in preparing to become a missionary. How impossible it had all seemed to me, but all God asked me to do was to try, and then He worked. The government was paying all of my tuition and was giving me subsistence money. I was free to give my full time to study. I felt as if God had brought me to school.

Very soon after beginning his schoolwork in the autumn of 1945, DeShazer was being called to so many points as a featured speaker that it almost disrupted his school program.

He bought an automobile and frequently took other students to various Christian services, particularly where he was to participate. At times, however, he was ready to let others know something of his experiences and also some of his inner problems:

It was a great change from the life I had been living in a Japanese war prison. Everyone on the campus called me "Jake." It seemed that they all knew me since my name and pictures had been in the papers. I tried to remember the other students' names, but it seemed difficult to remember all of them. However, they were all my friends, and I enjoyed their friendship very much.

He was greatly interested in his speaking engagements. At the same time he felt a great urge to accelerate his school program as much as possible. As his first year of school moved along and he learned there would be a summer session, he made plans to complete his total four-year college course in three calendar years. Since the government was paying all of his expenses and since he had a modest bank account, he really wanted for nothing. Such were his plans early in 1946. These plans, however, were intensified and given much more meaning after he began to share his desires and plans with a lovely Christian young woman, also a student at Seattle Pacific College.

14.   Romance and Marriage

Early in the spring of 1946 DeShazer went to a Youth for Christ service with Miss Florence Matheny. This young lady, a few years younger than DeShazer, was a junior in college. She had come to Seattle Pacific in the fall of 1945, from Toddville, Iowa, after completing her first two years in Lenox Junior College. Notwithstanding the fact that one was a freshman and the other a junior, these two were often seen together. As might be expected they felt a common purpose. In describing her, DeShazer in retrospect says:

> She was a very attractive young lady, the most attractive young lady I had ever met, and she wanted to go into full-time work for the Lord. We both felt a oneness of purpose, and when I asked Miss Matheny if she would marry me, she said that she would. When we prayed to Jesus, we felt that He would be pleased to give us a life together.

At the close of the summer school in 1946, Jake and Florence went to Gresham, Oregon, where on August 29, they were married. The ceremony was performed by Florence's former pastor, the Reverend J. K. French. Much publicity was given to this event which took place approximately one year after DeShazer's release from prison. Over and over again he was known to say that he felt God fulfilling His promise as found in Proverbs 3:6, "In all thy ways acknowledge him, and he shall direct thy paths." Jake and Florence felt this was definitely true in connection with their courtship and marriage. They felt God had directed them in finding one another. Now the two went forward together with plans to tell the true God-given plan of salvation.

The calls for DeShazer to go on speaking engagements were just as numerous as they were during the year before. Now, however, Florence went along for many of these meetings. The two young people seemed to get along in a wonderful way. Jake's message of love based upon his prison experiences and Florence's message of consecration to missionary endeavor seemed to touch the hearts and minds of every audience. People enjoyed having them in their homes. Youth groups enjoyed their testimonies. Many were the decisions for Christ, and many were the dedications to missionary service.

When at home, they read the Bible and prayed together at least twice every day. Over and over they emphasized the value of their little family altar. They said they had dedicated their time, their strength, and their possessions to the Lord.

A new experience came to DeShazer on the last day of October 1947. He attended his classes but seemed to be living out of this world. Other students greeted him with congratulations and this big question, "Is it a boy or a girl?" It was not long, however, until everyone knew that the new baby, born at eight-thirty that morning, was a bouncing, eight-pound-seven-ounce boy and the very image of his mother.

DeShazer announced that they were going to call the lad Paul Edward, with the further statement, "The Paul is after the apostle Paul, and I don't know where the Edward came from." The dad was rather free in the distribution of candy bars.

Between visits to the hospital DeShazer was trying to study and attend classes. For the first time, however, he was spending his evenings alone at the veterans' unit at 2585 Third Avenue West, just about six blocks up the hill from the college. He admitted he had a lot of time for study but made the further comment, "It is rather hard to concentrate."

From that time on, Deshazer was a typical doting dad. Seldom could he make a public statement without telling something about his boy, Paul, and it was rather difficult to get a picture of him alone without the baby.

During the remainder of the school year Florence stayed at home to take care of Paul. She had only eight credits more of schoolwork in order to finish her bachelor of arts degree. Since Jake himself would have to go to school the following summer, they agreed to finish their work together during the summer.

15.   From College To Japan

By special dispensation on the part of the college faculty, Jake and Florence were allowed to go through the regular graduation exercises in June 1948, even though it was necessary for both of them to do further work subsequently in the summer session.

Following the formal graduation, things moved very rapidly with respect to the DeShazers. They had already been accepted as outgoing missionaries to Japan by the Missionary Board of the Free Methodist Church of North America. Many calls came for them in this connection to do deputation work, to meet with various groups, and to make definite plans for going to the Orient. Many other groups, including Youth for Christ, young people's summer camps, the Bible Meditation League, church conferences, and others were sending in calls for them. In addition to this, of course, was a full summer school schedule for Jake and a partial summer session load for Florence. A niece of Jake, Elaine Blackwell, assisted in caring for little Paul. This summer school work, however, was done with high acceptability. Thus, in three calendar years, he had completed a regular four-year college course including nine credits through military training, a total of one hundred eighty-six quarter credits. He received the bachelor of arts degree with a major in missions. Florence also received the bachelor of arts degree with a major in missions.

It was now almost the first of September, and the couple was hoping to sail soon after the first of November. The maritime strike, however, made it impossible for them to sail until December 14.

For an eight-day period in September, Jake and Florence had charge of one of the booths at the Third World Missions Conference which was held on the campus of Seattle Pacific College. About one hundred missionaries were present to participate in this conference. Between fifty and sixty different missions and missionary boards were represented.

At the conclusion of the conference, the little family started on a speaking tour of the United States. This was somewhat of any eye-opener for Jake, for he found there was great enthusiasm throughout America for promoting Christian missions in Japan. There seemed to be a feeling everywhere that the doors of Japan were open wide to the gospel. They toured east and then south and returned west to Los Angeles and San Francisco.

Here they boarded the U.S.S. *General Meigs* and left San Francisco December 14, 1948, just six years and eight months after he had gone on the

U.S.S. *Hornet* under the Golden Gate Bridge, April 2, 1942. Almost exactly half of the intervening time he had spent in prison. The *General Meigs* was a rough-riding ship. There was a total of sixteen people in the cabin where Florence and Paul stayed. Most of these other people were missionaries. These included Miss Alice Fensome, another Free Methodist missionary, who was making her first trip to Japan.

The ship docked for a day or two at Honolulu, thus making it possible for the DeShazers to meet the parents of several students they had known in college. They spoke at one of the churches, for one of the docking days was Sunday. They left the Honolulu harbor Sunday night. A large crowd gathered and sang gospel songs as the boat pulled away.

While making this two-week-trip, DeShazer, of course, had many thoughts. Some of these he has written down:

> This time I was not going as a bombardier, but I was going as a missionary. Now I had love and good intentions toward Japan. How much better it is to go out to conquer evil with the gospel of peace! The strength and power must come from God, but God's promise is, "I have set before thee an open door, and no man can shut it" (Revelation 3:8). I have tried God's promises out in the past, and God always keeps his promises.
>
> My brave little wife was ready for the fight. There might be hardship and trouble, but there would be no turning back on her part. This is God's battle and God says, "Be not afraid nor dismayed by reason of this great multitude." To fight with God gives confidence and victory, and the victory will be glorious. People who find Jesus are never sorry. Jesus gives a better life in this world and the sure promise of eternal joy in the next. We are going to Japan to tell about Jesus and show the way of peace and happiness. We hope to see Japan become a Christian nation that Japan may be among the nations that have the joy of worshipping before the true God.

16.   First Experiences as Missionary

More than one million tracts concerning the Doolittle raider who turned missionary had been distributed throughout Japan. This tract in Japanese contained a blank to be signed by those who would accept Jesus Christ as their Saviour. Many thousands of these were signed and returned. In view of this, the name, DeShazer, was known to many Japanese people. So it was that on December 28, 1948, when DeShazer and his little family arrived in Yokohama docks, crowds were waiting to see him. Many were anxious to know the cause of the change of attitude of a man who had been held for many months by the Japanese in a solitary cell. They could not understand how one's heart once filled with animosity could now be overflowing with love for his persecutors.

As they pressed around DeShazer and asked many questions, he felt at first quite helpless. He knew he had been "born again," but he also knew that an expression like that meant very little to people who did not know the Bible. It did not take long, however, for him to commit the problem to the Lord. He says:

> By myself I was helpless. For flesh and blood cannot reveal the great spiritual truths. It is God that reveals and saves, and we must have God's forgiving, tender spirit in order for God to use us. If God will use us, even children can understand, and people who have put their trust in man-made idols will turn from idolatry and put their trust in the true and living God.

Troubles and disappointment were not slow in coming. The DeShazers had been taken by friends to an American-style house, but there was little heat in the house, and these newcomers from America felt damp and cold. The next day little Paul was ill with a bad cold. Jake had already accepted an appointment to speak at the Suginami Free Methodist Church in Tokyo on the next Sunday. The baby's cold became worse, and the house seemed to be extremely cold. By Saturday they began to look for a doctor. They finally learned that they could take Paul to an army hospital.

Here the doctor checked the baby carefully and said he should be left at the hospital where it was warmer and where he could be given medical care. This was a hard blow to Florence. How could she leave the little fellow in the hospital and not be near him for a week? They were able, however, to commit their situation to the Lord, particularly the case of little

Paul. DeShazer says:

> It was good to know Jesus at that time and to realize that He knows all about us and our every problem. When we committed our lives to Jesus, we had given everything. We would venture our lives for Jesus' sake that the precious gospel might bring peace and joy. The time of testing had come, but we must not turn back now; "No man, having put his hand to the plow, and looking back, is fit for the kingdom of God" (Luke 9:62).

A week later Florence was able to go back to the hospital and see Paul. He seemed to be improving. On this same Saturday, Jake visited two churches in Tokyo, the Suginami and the Oji. As an interpreter he had Dr. Kaneo Oda, also a graduate of Seattle Pacific College.

It was a great joy to DeShazer to be in Japan and have the privilege of preaching the gospel. News concerning him had spread everywhere. Consequently, churches and halls were filled to capacity. DeShazer had used John 1:12 as a test many times. In this connection he asks people whether they are willing to receive Jesus. In response many hundreds are quick to indicate their decision to try out the promises of God in order that they may receive the gift of eternal life.

In due time, their overseas baggage arrived in Yokohama. A splendid gentleman, Mr. Yoshiki, arranged for them to live upstairs in his home. Here it was that they set up their big oil stove which they had brought from America. They also dug out of their baggage cans of milk for baby Paul. It was only a few days after being able to have this proper food that Paul was running about as if he had never been sick.

Florence, herself, started to hold Bible classes in her own home. Many people were coming to see them, particularly in the evening. As a result both Jake and Florence were holding classes for instruction. To do this, of course, meant they needed an interpreter, for notwithstanding all the study they had made in the Japanese language in America, they were not about to converse readily in this foreign tongue. Finally they settled down to one class between them with a very faithful Christian, helpful as an interpreter. This was Mr. Nishidi, whose work during the day was interpreting for Japanese representatives of the U.S. Military Police. After about two months, Florence had to take over all of the evening classes because Jake was out most of the time on speaking tours. Within a few weeks, five people from Mr. Yoshiki's home were baptized as Christians. Many others declared their intention of accepting Christ.

Within a few months after his arrival in Japan, DeShazer had spoken in nearly two hundred different places. Since then the number has continued to grow. Because it seemed almost impossible to get back immediately to the same place a second time, he made it a point always to call for decisions at his very first meeting.

Under the leadership of the Holy Spirit and the light of His Word, many people who had been living lives of sin suddenly turned about-face and with new courage were living Christian lives. Reports were coming to DeShazer in large numbers regarding the inspiration his messages had brought and expressing a determination to live the Christian way. The following is a sample of such letters. This was received from a young lady who indicates something of the joy she has had in her newfound experience.

On the sixteenth of May I received new life through the message which you gave. Thank you. While you were talking I cried very much. Through your prisoner-of-war life, you have had a great deal of hatred toward the Japanese people. They were cruel in their treatment of you. I know that you have unreasonable treatment through their ignorance. I know that some Japanese are very impolite and uncultivated. Please forgive us. I have no words to apologize for our rudeness.

However, you have forgiven us, and you came to Japan to save us. I could not help but cry to think of the love which God has put in your heart. I was a very sinful girl. I told a lie many times, but now I have repented. I have had much trouble since becoming a Christian. Before I was a Christian, I must support my family who were in poor condition. I have three brothers and parents, and I had health while they were sick. I worked as a factory girl, but I was very discouraged. I tried to kill myself three or four tines, but without success. I just couldn't go through with suicide. I didn't have any affection toward Japan, and I had little interest. I started working at the public welfare section as a case worker.

I always hated God, and I had contracted the sickness of heart beriberi. I quit my work, but after a week I found a circular of your coming to our town to make a speech. I attended the meeting. And the sixteenth of May will always be a memorial day as well as a revolutionary day for me. By you I was reborn as a child is born on earth. I was now a child born in the heavenly kingdom. Now, "The Lord is my life and my salvation; whom shall I fear?"

Thank you very much for what you have done. I am full of hope and optimism for the future. I am learning a university course by correspondence. It will take two more years to finish this course, and then I have a hope to go and learn more of God in your country. That is only a hope, now. Please pray for me and my hope.

I hope that I can attend your next meeting near our town.

Please give my kindest regards to Mrs. DeShazer and Mr. Oda. May God bless you.

DeShazer gives testimony in regard to such experiences:

> It is a great joy to know that God has redeemed souls who are lost. They will rejoice throughout eternity. Glory be to God who alone is to be praised. One girl told me that her sweetheart lost his life in the raid of which I was a participant. She heard about me through pamphlets and newspaper articles, and she made up her mind that she was going to have the pleasure of taking revenge on me by killing me if it were possible. This attractive young lady came to one service which we held, and to her surprise the Spirit of Jesus showed her how wrong her intentions had been. She determined to seek this Spirit of love which Jesus gives and God wonderfully helped her. I have seen her many times since that time, and the sweet look on her face is truly convincing of the power of Jesus to change a person's life from hatred to love. What a pleasure it is to strive for peace in this Christian way rather than to come with airplanes, bombs, and guns. How much more lasting will this Christian method of peace be than the method of war and hatred!

In the spring of 1949, nearly four years after the war's end, one of the strangest meetings that has ever happened was DeShazer's happy experience at the O.S.S. Theatre in Osaka, Japan. By prearrangement many of the people in Japan who had lost loved ones during the war and as many of the Japanese guards as possible met on the platform of the big theater with DeShazer and his wife. An unusual spirit of forgiveness seemed to pervade the entire place. DeShazer spoke to the large audience telling them about the message of forgiveness that Jesus preached nearly two thousand years ago. He told them that both they and he had been in the bitter anguish of the terrible war. "But now," he said, "we see the right thing to do is to forgive, to love one another, and to work together for one another's happiness."

He told them about Jesus as God's Son and about the Holy Spirit who is able to bring light and truth. Two men, Mr. Aota and Mr. Misaka, DeShazer's prison guards, expressed their desire to become Christians. These men had been reading the Bible themselves and showing a very splendid attitude. DeShazer says, "We are praying, not only for my former guard, but for the Spirit of Christ to spread to all of the people in Japan so that the whole nation will become a Christian nation."

17.   Forty-Day Fast and Expanding Ministry

Early in 1950, with impending war in Korea and continued Communistic infiltration in Japan despite General MacArthur's ban on communism, DeShazer felt a burden for further self-analysis and Spirit-anointing if his ministry was to reach the highest possible level of effectiveness. Then, too, it seemed to him that the immediate evangelism of all Japan was so imperative it could not wait for the normal operations of the various missionary boards. A miracle or series of miracles would be necessary if Japan was to be saved from communism on the one hand and from a cold, philosophical, and impotent Christianity on the other. Such a miracle, he felt, could come to pass only through prayer and fasting.

Thus it was that DeShazer entered upon a forty-day fast. He did not withdraw from active evangelistic work, nor did he stop his language study. During the entire period he ate practically nothing. For the first three days he went without water as well as food. After that, on the advice of friends, he permitted himself to have water. He would not permit himself even to have fruit juices.

There was no thought on DeShazer's part of doing something spectacular. Rather, he felt a divine urge to pray for a spiritual awakening throughout all Japan.

Many Christians as well as non-Christians were greatly impressed by DeShazer's fast. A reporter for one of the leading Japanese newspapers told Bob Pierce, of Youth for Christ, that DeShazer's fast had produced a profound effect upon the Japanese people. He suggested that DeShazer had already won the friendship of the Japanese by returning as a missionary. Now he was even fasting for them! They had been accustomed to the fastings of the Buddhist priests but seldom or never had they known of a foreign missionary fasting. The reporter further stated that there were many things about Christianity they could not understand but that they could understand DeShazer, and they liked him.

Within a week after the termination of his fast, seven different Christian ministers called on DeShazer to inquire regarding fasting as a Christian activity. Evidently they, too, had a heart hunger for more of God.

DeShazer reports that his fasting was a very rewarding experience. From that time on, God has been answering his prayer. One of the first evidences was the conversion on April 14, 1950, of Captain Mitsuo Fuchida, commander of the three hundred sixty planes of the Japanese air squadron which bombed Pearl Harbor on that fateful December 7, 1941. His conversion was a tangible demonstration of God's miracle-working power. Fuchida has written the wonder story of his conversion in tract form which has been distributed widely by the Pocket Testament League.

The tract tells about the unique manner in which God used DeShazer's testimony *I Was a Prisoner of Japan* (a tract published by the Bible Meditation League) to bring Fuchida under conviction. Within a month after his conversion, he had the privilege of being with DeShazer in a great mass meeting in the largest auditorium in Osaka, where both men gave their testimonies. At least four thousand people had been crowded into the auditorium, and as many as three thousand were outside unable to enter. At the close of the meeting approximately five hundred individuals came down the aisles as seekers for the Christian way of life.

DeShazer continues to preach the gospel. It would be easy for him to let up until the Christian people of America "prayed down" a revival for Japan. But no, he is giving himself without stint.

Soon after the conversion of Fuchida, DeShazer with his chief interpreter, the Reverend Dr. Kaneo Oda, began extensive evangelistic tours. They spent a month or more with the coal miners on Kyushu Island. Here they held two meetings a day with an average attendance of one thousand or more. Opportunity was given for those interested to remain after each service for prayer. Many thus remained, the number in several instances reaching as high as four hundred. From Kyushu they went to Hiroshima, the city of the atom bomb, for a series of meetings.

As this printed biographical story concludes, DeShazer and Oda with a Gospel Sound Truck are making a tour of the coal mines of Hokkaido. With the mounted public-address system they are holding many street meetings. Gospel literature in large quantities is being distributed. God is blessing in a most gracious way. The work and the marvelous life of DeShazer goes forward!

Epilogue

by *Leona K. Fear*

In the years that followed the Japanese surrender, many thousands of Japanese heard the gospel message from the lips of Jake DeShazer. Many came out of curiosity to see the man who had suffered so much but had come back to live among them as a witness to God's love. Some came to inquire the way of salvation. Others came with hearts full of hatred for the American who represented to them the devastation of war, the loss of loved ones, and the humiliation of defeat.

Crowds came to DeShazer's home in Osaka, a house that had been provided by a Japanese man whose son was killed in the war. There was little or no privacy. The owner of the house feared for the life of his friend and arranged with the police department for the erection of a police box by the gate of the DeShazer home. Every night the area was patrolled. And yet, DeShazer walked among the people, smiling and unafraid.

Those who came to the DeShazer home were welcomed. Mrs. DeShazer, with the help of an interpreter, began Bible classes in their living room. Attendance increased. The room was packed out. Many were converted.

Jake continued in a country-wide evangelism. His ministry reached to the northern island of Hokkaido and southwest to the southernmost island of Kyushu. People were so responsive to the gospel and so many calls came that it was difficult to find time for language study. Although DeShazer could not speak Japanese, he spoke the language of love, a language readily understood by the Japanese people. A fellow missionary remembers DeShazer with a group of young Japanese high school boys. He tried to speak to them in a few broken words of Japanese mixed with English which they could not understand. But when he gently placed a hand on their shoulders and they saw the look of love in his amazing blue eyes, they were melted to tears.

Among those who came during the evangelistic rallies was a young girl. DeShazer says that she "watched me so constantly that she began to make me self-conscious." In order to break the spell DeShazer offered to help her. She hurried away without speaking, but not before DeShazer saw intense hatred and open hostility reflected in her eyes. She came again to the next meeting where DeShazer recounted his prison experiences. He emphasized that God had changed his hatred for the Japanese people to love.

The girl listened intently, caught up in the drama of a life transformed by the power of Christ. She came again and again. In the weeks that followed she became one of the most enthusiastic members of a group that frequently met in the DeShazer home for informal discussion sessions.

One night she told her story. She confessed that she had first come to the meetings with the avowed purpose of killing DeShazer. She had sworn vengeance against the American bombardier because her sweetheart had been killed in the war. But that night DeShazer had spoken of his own hatred having been changed to love. That message of God's love worked the same change inside her as it had in DeShazer in the prison camp. Her life was transformed. She was now a Christian.

DeShazer had a deep appreciation and respect for Dr. Kaneo Oda, who accompanied him in evangelistic rallies throughout Japan. Dr. Oda was not only a dedicated Christian minister but an excellent interpreter. Usually he gave a short introduction before DeShazer spoke. Jake reports with a bit of wry humor that "at first the introductions were short, but finally they became very long. Indeed, sometimes I noticed that it took one hour for Oda to finish his introductory remarks."

A deep spiritual bond existed between the two -- the short, kindly, Japanese intellectual and the gentle American missionary with the winning smile and the simple faith. DeShazer gives us an insight into that relationship, "Oda and I spent weeks and months together. Usually we would stay at a pastor's home for the night. Sometimes we would be at a missionary's home, and at other times a company would keep us in their lovely club house. In Japanese homes we would always take a bath. They do not, or at that time they didn't, furnish towels. Since I usually forgot to take my own personal towel, Oda let me use his. The towel would be a small one, for he didn't want to pack a big bath towel. Soon the small towel would be wet, and we would wring it out. I was embarrassed, of course, since it was not mine and would always ask Oda to use the towel first. Sometimes in Oda's long introductions I could understand enough Japanese to realize that he was talking about the towel." Jake continues, "Oda was my good friend. My love for the Japanese people was deep and sincere. I know that it came from God."

In 1951 the DeShazers asked for and received a miracle -- the healing of their small son, Paul, from encephalitis. In September Paul had become critically ill and was taken to the army hospital where in spite of all skilled doctors and nurses could do for him, he slipped into a coma. Mrs. DeShazer says, "During those crisis hours the Lord sustained Jake and me in a wonderful way. Even as I prayed, the song came to me: 'Let all them that put their trust in thee rejoice, rejoice.'" Other Christian friends were praying, both in Japan and at home. God answered prayer. Paul wakened from the coma that he had been in for many days completely whole, although everyone had warned of possible brain damage which could manifest itself in muscular paralysis or mental retardation. "It is a miracle," was the report of the doctors and nurses who attended Paul. "He is the worst case of sleeping sickness that we have ever had, but he has made the quickest and most complete recovery." The DeShazers had come to expect miracles from God, and God honored their simple faith.

DeShazer continued to receive many calls for evangelistic services, but he felt that in order to consolidate the results of his ministry, new places of worship should be opened. With this in mind he began to hold services each Thursday night in a large storage room at Amami, one of the poorer areas of south Osaka. Among those who assisted him with the services was a young high school student. One day the young man introduced DeShazer to a man who before his conversion had been a drunkard and a Buddhist priest. He told DeShazer that upon his conversion he had thrown his idols out in the yard and stomped them in the dust. He wept as he testified of God's redeeming love.

At Amami, DeShazer also met Arimoto, a cripple, who became a Christian when he read an account of Jake's experience in the newspaper. Although paralysis had left Arimoto with a speech defect, he could write and he could pray. He was able to enlist the help of influential people. He lived a steady, Christian life. DeShazer describes him as "the strong one."

Dr. Oda was impressed by the work in Amami and urged the church members and students at Osaka Christian College to give assistance to the project.

The DeShazer family moved into a new home near the site of Osaka Christian College. From this home base DeShazer continued to extend his ministry. In the coal mines of Japan, in factories, on the streets, in theaters, in schools, in tent meetings, in their own home, and in churches -- DeShazer used every opportunity to proclaim God's love. A report of his activities for the month of March, 1951, indicates the scope of his ministry:

1.   Each morning of the weekdays from eight o'clock are spent in language study. We seem to be making some progress lately, but I haven't preached in the Japanese language yet.

2.   Sermons preached for past month were - 40.

3.   People reached - 6,500.

4.   Quantity of literature distributed: Gospel of John - 6,000; pamphlets - 10,000.

5.   Decisions to accept Christ - 505.

6.   Baptisms - helped baptize - 14.

7.   Miles traveled - around 350.

The rich and the poor, the high and the low were touched by the DeShazer testimony. The maid in their home was converted. Those in the emperor's palace heard the story. At the invitation of the royal household DeShazer went to Tokyo and was received by Prince Takamatsu, brother of the emperor. In characteristic simplicity Deshazer describes the incident, "I did not know what to do in the presence of royalty. I was fortunate to be with Colonel Hill, and I followed his example. He went in and shook the prince's hand and said, 'How do you do?' We then sat down, and a servant brought us tea and cakes. I was glad for the opportunity to give the message of the Christian hope to Prince Takamatsu. I also expressed my thanks to the prince for the emperor's mercy in sparing my life during the war."

DeShazer's ministry reached far beyond the bounds of the island kingdom of Japan. In October 1952 at the invitation of the United States Armed Forces he conducted a two-week preaching mission among the Air Force men in Korea. Special permission was given for him to visit some of the restricted war zones. He traveled eight hundred sixty miles by jeep, truck, airplane, and helicopter during the two-week period. When not preaching, he could be found chatting with the men and counseling them. He was popular with the airmen wherever he went. A high point of his Korean ministry was the opportunity to preach in a large Protestant church which had been built entirely by North Korean refugees. Approximately one thousand Koreans and servicemen attended. He learned that many of the Korean Christians had walked great distances to attend the service. The building was without heat, but there was a warmth of spirit which was contagious. Saints clapped their hands and shouted, "Amen," in response to DeShazer's message. It was a heartwarming experience for DeShazer.

The DeShazers had a great interest in Osaka Christian College. In March, 1953, revival swept across the campus, and DeShazer was a part of it. There were times of confession of sin and genuine repentance. DeShazer prayed with every student. One who was there said, "Even though I could not understand him, I could feel love."

DeShazer himself wrote, "The seminary students are all hoarse from nearly eleven days of shouting and praying and weeping for joy. We can hardly take time to eat or sleep or write letters. At one church we shouted and praised God and wept for joy all day."

Wonderful things happened as the revival swept throughout the college, the churches, and other missions in the area. DeShazer tells the story of a woman, converted during those meetings, who was set upon by bandits who tried to kill her. A knife, the murder weapon, had cut into her pocket New Testament as far as the book of Romans when a patrol car arrived and she was rescued by the police. One of the young men who had been greatly used of the Spirit during the revival was taken by illness and death only two months later. Prior to his death he had brought both of his parents to the Lord. He had also given a Bible to a seeker who accepted Christ. After the young man's death DeShazer had the joy of baptizing the new convert.

DeShazer described the revival as the greatest movement of the Spirit he had ever seen. "Sick are healed, demons cast out, storms stilled, people filled with the Holy Spirit, sins confessed, and the glory of the Lord manifested many times. Many people have been converted."

In April of that year DeShazer returned to the United States to meet for a reunion with the Doolittle flyers. He used this opportunity to travel extensively for a month, holding rallies in North American churches. As the humble, Spirit-filled missionary brought news of revival in Japan, revival came to America. DeShazer spoke almost every night and often twice each day in college centers, churches, and interdenominational gatherings. Scores of young people were challenged to dedicated their lives to Christ. Many opened their hearts to the work of the Holy Spirit.

Tireless in his efforts to get the gospel out to the Japanese people as quickly and extensively as possible, DeShazer decided in 1954 to launch a radio broadcast. Many were contacted through this ministry. From one station, in six months' time two hundred ninety-one enrolled in Bible correspondence courses. One station manager liked the program so much that he sent it out on two other stations at no cost. The radio ministry penetrated even into Buddhist temples and reached young men who were training to be priests. In spite of the fact that at one time Jake turned over the remaining two thousand dollars of his prison pay and sold his camera to keep the program on the air, the ministry continued to be in financial straits. It was necessary to take the program off the air.

The DeShazers were then living in Nishinomiya in the home of a wealthy man, manufacturer of bean curd, who had offered the place to them rent free. Upstairs was a large room which had been used as a dance hall. This, the DeShazers determined, should be used for a Sunday school and church. Mrs. DeShazer began to gather in the neighborhood children for felt-o-gram pictures and Bible stories. About sixty children met each Sunday in the DeShazer home. The living room couch held children on four levels - a row on the floor, in front of the couch, one row on the edge, one against the back, and the fourth row on top. The old couch has been known to hold as many as thirteen or more youngsters. Fourteen new converts were baptized the first year in Nishinomiya. From this nucleus of believers came the church which the DeShazers had envisioned. Other workers followed the DeShazers at Nishinomiya and built upon the foundation which had been laid through the early Bible studies held in the DeShazer home. In May of 1958 a Free Methodist church was dedicated in Nishinomiya. Among those who joined the newly formed congregation was a Mr. Tanaka, a mat maker, who had been one of the early converts.

At the close of the year 1954 the DeShazers had been in Japan for six years. The great interest in Christianity which had followed World War II was waning. Jake wrote, "We enroll many people in a Bible study course and it seems quite easy to win souls to the Lord, but the number of Christians in Japan does not increase very fast. The Japanese seem to enjoy Christianity for a while, but their family ties are strong, the Buddhist priests are powerful, and the government seems in favor of their old forms of worship. Then, too, the Japanese are very proud of their culture."

Yet in the closing year of his first term of service, 1954, he reported more than thirty-five hundred people had made decisions to accept Christ within the twelve-month period. Typical of those persons responding was a young Japanese who was handed a tract on the street one day. As a result of that contact he came to the DeShazer home for Bible study. Soon afterwards he confessed Christ as Saviour and began to lead others to Christ. He brought DeShazer to his high school and arranged for him to speak to about four hundred students. As a result DeShazer was invited to begin a Bible class at the school.

In April of 1955 the DeShazers returned to the United States for furlough. They had arrived in Japan with one child - baby Paul. Three other children had been born to them in Japan - John, Mark, and Carol. While Jake had been engaged in active evangelism and the work of mission superintendent, his wife, Florence, had carried on nobly not only as wife and mother to a young family, but by teaching classes at Osaka Christian College and conducting children's meetings and English Bible study groups in their home. For six and one half years they had carried on extensive evangelistic efforts, and thousands of Japanese had heard the story of God's love from the former Doolittle flyer.

DeShazer not only had spoken of God's love but had exemplified it as he walked among the Japanese people. He was greatly concerned about the fate of the Japanese war criminals and pleaded for mercy on their behalf. He remembered with gratitude that the emperor of Japan had intervened for him when he was under the sentence of death. He wrote, "I owe the emperor of Japan an eternal debt of gratitude. I would have spent eternity in hell if I had been executed at that time, for I was not a Christian." He pleaded, "Our country was the first to drop the atomic bomb, now let us be the first to show mercy."

Upon the return of the family to the United States, DeShazer was much in demand as a speaker in churches, camps, and rallies. However, he felt it would do the missionary cause more good if he could spend three years in Asbury, and in the fall of 1955 he enrolled in the seminary program.

The DeShazer story continued to go out both through Jake's own ministry and through the secular press. In November of 1956 the DeShazer story was presented over nationwide television. The thirty-minute program,

"The Return of the Bombardier," was performed by professional actors for DuPont Cavalcade Theater and portrayed the story of Jake's imprisonment, his conversion, and his return to Japan as an ambassador of God's love.

In the spring of 1958 DeShazer completed a three-year study program at Asbury Theological Seminary, graduating with a bachelor of divinity degree.

In late December the DeShazers were ready to return to Japan. Their five children accompanied them - Paul, John, Mark, Carol, and little Ruth, who was just a few months old.

It was a thrilling experience to be back on Japanese soil after a three year absence. The DeShazers rejoiced to greet old friends and to find those who were standing true in their Christian faith. At one of the churches they visited, ten people stood saying that they had been brought to the Lord because of DeShazer's ministry.

Among those who found their way to the DeShazer home during their first few weeks back in Japan was a former suicide pilot. The man had amazingly survived seven airplane crashes during the war and many, many serious injuries. This young man had sought out DeShazer, only a short time before they left for America, to ask him to perform his marriage ceremony. At that time neither he nor his bride-to-be were Christians. There, in the DeShazer home, both had knelt and accepted Christ. At the wedding ceremony some of the kamikaze (divine wind) friends of the groom had sung military songs. The Christians sang hymns. Now, four years later, the kamikaze pilot came to DeShazer for baptism -- he had been waiting for DeShazer's return to Japan. He invited DeShazer to his home where eight or ten people were regularly meeting for Bible study. No wonder DeShazer wrote, "This surely is an interesting life since Christ became real to me."

DeShazer now looked to the Japanese church leaders for guidance as to his future role in the church. The work of the missionary in the years ahead, DeShazer discovered, would be that of church building. Jake felt that his particular calling was to pioneer new churches. He planned to stay a year or two at a new location in order to start a church and then be ready to move on to another locality, leaving the new church in the capable hands of a Japanese pastor.

It was agreed that the family should locate in Nagoya, the city which Jake helped to bomb. He wrote home to his mission board, "Why should we not go out where we can work and others cannot? Nagoya is exactly the right place for us!"

A survey of the area led them to an outlying district of Nagoya, the town of Moriyama. There were no Christian churches in Moriyama. It was a growing city. New homes were going up, and bridges were being built. In a year or two the district would be incorporated within the greater city of Nagoya, a city of sixty thousand population. In a section called Smith Town they found several American-style houses which had been built during the American occupation. It seemed a good starting point.

To DeShazer it seemed like a dream come true to be able to move into the city he had once bombed to proclaim the love of God. In May of 1959 the DeShazer family were in their new home and ready to go to work. They began by making friends with their Japanese neighbors. They brought children into the home for Bible stories. They distributed Christian literature. They taught English Bible classes. In September when a typhoon hit the area they extended a helping hand to those who suffered the loss of loved ones and personal possessions. The DeShazers themselves had lost part of the roof of their home in the storm. The board fence surrounding the home blew down on the neighbor's house. Books, bedding, and clothing were soaked. Electricity was off. Many houses in Moriyama, however, had fared much worse - some had been completely flattened, many had been flooded. Those standing unprotected were being looted. The DeShazers shared what they could with their needy neighbors.

Approximately one year after moving to Nagoya, August, 1960, they reported that five new members had been received into the church, bringing the total membership to twenty-one. Meetings were still being held in the DeShazer home. One of those who came was a layman, Mr. Gotoh, who had been a member of Miss Ruth Mylander's Bible class before the war. Now he was vice-president of a large automobile manufacturing company and was living in the Nagoya area. He was a great help to the DeShazers. He attended regularly and took Jake's place in the pulpit every third Sunday.

Among the new converts was a young man, a commercial student, who attended the English Bible class. He had studied all the religions of Japan, but neither Shinto nor Buddhism satisfied his quest for forgiveness of sins. He heard the gospel message only a few times and gave his heart to Christ. Following graduation he began working in a bank. He was a faithful worker in the Nagoya church, organizing the young people's society and assisting with the Sunday school work.

In 1963, DeShazer wrote that land had been purchased and money was available for a church building. Four years of hard work and faithful sowing of the seed had come to fruition. With the building of the new church, DeShazer's work had been accomplished. The congregation was turned over to a Japanese pastor. The DeShazers were now ready to return to America for furlough.

Family needs and other circumstances kept the DeShazers at home for three and one-half years. During this time the family moved to a farm in Oregon, and DeShazer once more became a man of the soil. Although he was not engaged in a full-time Christian ministry, his testimony continued to make an impact both in the home churches and in Japan. A mid-western conference superintendent reported in 1964: "We have just closed our five-day meeting with DeShazer - a time of genuine revival in every sense of the word. . . . The night we showed the film we had to borrow chairs. . . . [There were] six first-time converts . . . many filled with the Spirit . . . [and] a spirit of renewal and rededication through the entire church."

In 1966 DeShazer wrote, "We are working on a film with Mitsuo Fuchida. I think the film will have great evangelistic possibilities. It would have more meaning for Japanese than for Americans."

Then in September of 1967 the Oregon farm with its flock of sheep and crops of cucumbers were left behind as the DeShazers finished their second furlough and turned once more toward Japan. It was exciting to see what the Lord had been doing during their absence. It was a joy to once more be reunited with Japanese friends. DeShazer reported, "More than twenty new churches had developed since we came to Japan. The progress is slow, but we thank God for the new churches and the plan for more new churches." He found that the Nagoya church, which he had left, was making plans to build over the top of the original building. It was an encouragement to know that the people who had been converted under the DeShazer ministry were standing true and growing in Christian experience. After years of working in a bank, Mr. Sasakawa, the young man who had been one of the first converts at Nagoya, entered college to study law. By doing so he hoped to have a greater opportunity to mingle with college students and present them with the Christian message. He was holding five-minute appointed talks with students concerning Christ and salvation. New inquirers were attending church because of his witness.

DeShazer had returned to Japan still convinced that the most effective way to accomplish missionary work was to concentrate on getting new churches started. Once more he placed himself in the hands of the Japanese church for assignment. The Evangelism Committee of the Japan Free Methodist Church had already voted to begin work in the city of Katsuta, a new area designed for commuter homes. Katsuta was located about one hundred miles from Tokyo and near to the great industrial city of Hitachi where a Free Methodist church is located. Missionary Norman Overland had begun the work in Katsuta before returning to America for furlough. On the advice of the Japanese conference, the DeShazer family moved to Hitachi and from this base of operations began evangelistic work in Katsuta, assisting the Japanese pastor who had been appointed to serve the area. With characteristic enthusiasm Jake traveled regularly to the Katsuta area where he conducted English Bible classes and Sunday services. DeShazer and the pastor visited homes, gave out tracts, and sold Bibles.

In 1968 a building was ready for services - really just a pastor's home with one big room for services. The believers previously had been meeting in one of the homes on Thursday morning and in one of the school buildings each Friday evening. With the dedication of the chapel-parsonage and with a resident pastor, DeShazer and the Japan Conference saw the accomplishment of the first project of a five-year plan for church expansion which they had adopted. Two years later, in October of 1971, DeShazer wrote, "Katsuta is planning to make a bigger building. I go to Katsuta once a month now to assist."

While continuing to live in Hitachi, DeShazer was appointed superintendent of the eastern conference of the Japan General Church, a responsibility he was reluctant to assume. "Pray for me," he wrote. "I don't know how to be a superintendent." He felt more at home conducting Bible studies, visiting in homes, passing out literature, and talking to his neighbor of the love of God.

In August of 1969, having seen the establishment of a sound work at Katsuta, DeShazer was ready for a new assignment. It had long been his dream to plant churches in the Tokyo area. Nishi Tokorozawa was the location chosen for the new evangelistic thrust, a town on the outskirts of Tokyo and outside the city limits. The DeShazers immediately began work. Evangelistic meetings were held in two kindergartens. Child evangelism classes were conducted in their home. By December of 1970 thirty children had made decisions for Christ. Adults have been reached. Sunday school and church services had been held in their home with a view of establishing another congregation. DeShazer's dream is coming true - Tokorozawa is becoming a new Christian center, a Christian witness in the great city of Tokyo. DeShazer hopes to see two more churches established in the Tokyo area.

Among those who had been reached is DeShazer's neighbor, Mr. Sato. In May, 1972, DeShazer wrote, "Each morning for some time I have been taking a walk with my neighbor. We go to a place called Hatchi Koku Yama, where there are many trees and green grass. The birds sound so sweet early in the morning from six to seven. We walk, and the talk is usually about the Bible and Christ. My neighbor, Mr. Sato, inherited his whiskey store from his father and makes a good living. He knows all the traditions of Japan. He told me this morning that he always wanted to believe in the kind of God that I talk about. He did not know, but felt that there must be a God who is One. He knew that God loves us, but he didn't know anything about the true Christian message until we came two years ago and told him. . . . Mr. Sato prays to Christ now, but he needs more fellowship and encouragement. It seems slow, but as we work and pray we remember Christ said, 'I have overcome the world.'"

The DeShazer story can never fully be told. Only eternity will reveal the impact of the life of the gentle, unassuming disciple of the Lord upon the land of Japan. Japanese people have gained new insight into the meaning of Christianity from this fair-skinned, blue-eyed man who walks among them with the common touch but imparts the divine touch of God. God's love reaches out through DeShazer to the Japanese people, and they respond. Jake says, "I love these beautiful Japanese people so much. They all look beautiful to me. They need Jesus."

The DeShazer story goes on and on. It lives through the ministry of Mitsuo Fuchida and through the ministry of a young Japanese who was converted when he heard Jake preach in his village. He and his wife are now telling the story of God's love in Brazil. The DeShazer story is lived out through the transformed lives of adults, children, and young people. Students, neighbors, and businessmen have been touched by it. North America, Japan, Korea, Brazil and the world have seen the love of God as shown in DeShazer's life and testimony. It continues to be told by DeShazer himself as he humbly seeks to tell all men of the love of God.

The DeShazer story is the account of one man who in simple transactions with God found the core of divine power at his fingertips - the transforming power of love.